To Ginny and

Jacque Griffin

She's
OUT THERE!

★ ★ ★ ★ ★

She's
OUT

The Next Generation of Presidential Candidates

ESSAYS BY 35 YOUNG WOMEN WHO ASPIRE TO LEAD THE NATION

THERE!

EDITED BY AMY SEWELL AND HEATHER L. OGILVIE
PHOTOGRAPHS BY ROBERT A. RIPPS

LIFETIME
MEDIA
NEW YORK

LifeTime Media, Inc.
352 Seventh Avenue
New York, NY 10001
Visit our Web site at www.lifetimemedia.com

ISBN: 978-0-9816368-4-9

Library of Congress Control Number: 2009925060

Designer: *Pauline Neuwirth, Neuwirth & Associates, Inc.*

All LifeTime Media titles are available for special promotions, premiums, and bulk purchase. For more information, please contact the manager of our special sales department at 212-631-7524 or sales@lifetimemedia.com

Distributed to the trade by Perseus Book Group

Printed in the United States of America
10 9 8 7 6 5 4 3 2 1

When people keep telling you that you can't do a
thing, you kind of like to try it.

—MARGARET CHASE SMITH, the first woman elected to
both the House of Representatives and the Senate, and the
first woman to have her name placed in nomination for
president at a major party's convention, at the 1964
Republican National Convention.

CONTENTS

APPENDIXES   201

FOREWORD

Since 1993, when I founded Take Our Daughters to Work, I have watched girls' growing expectations to be and do anything they choose. Many wrote to me that they intended to be president of the United States. They had no role models, of course, but that didn't stop them from dreaming. This is one of the reasons I started The White House Project in 1998—to get a diverse and critical mass of women into leadership, up to and including the presidency. Now, a decade after the WHP began its work, we saw a woman frontrunner vying for the nomination of a major party. Senator Hillary Rodham Clinton has permanently changed the options of girls and women. I doubt there will again be a presidential campaign without serious female candidates.

Clinton's run owes a debt to those who ran before her, brave and forward-looking women such as Shirley Chisholm, Patricia Schroeder, and Elizabeth Dole. They paved the way with guts and sweat, battling misogyny and disappointment, but the time was not right.

Now, 88 percent* of Americans say they are ready to vote for a woman president, and more than half the voters now feel a woman would do as good a job as—or better than— a man on the issues that have always kept females out of this executive post: foreign policy, homeland security, and the economy. Incidentally, they also feel a woman would do better on human rights and domestic issues.

It is our time, and the editors of this inspiring book, Amy Sewell and Heather L. Ogilvie, are right—the women who will reach the top are out there now. Most Americans may not know their names, but women governors and senators are in the pipeline to the presidency, and with Clinton's encouraging race, they will soon be stepping up. When you read this book, however, you will see how far down the pipeline extends. Girls as young as five plan to run, and some of the platforms they put forth in these essays are as sophisticated and moving as you will hear in a real campaign.

Seven-year-old Hannah L. Kuhn-Gale says that if she were president, she "would not like people to carry weapons around. They might kill people, and that is sort of like war." You wonder, reading her words, how a whole nation could lose its collective mind and not support gun control.

Ten-year-old Jacqueline Olivia Griffin knows what many women (sadly) still do not understand: "Politics affects everything." If she were president today, she "would try my hardest to stop the Iraq war. I would work with others to find a way to solve problems without war" (something she has already done as a peer mediator in her school). Ten-year-old Folasade Fayemi Kammen and eight-year-old Genevieve Greene Farley say that under their presidencies, the United States will take the lead on world environmental problems, especially global warming. Bring 'em on.

Finally, ten-year-old Hannah George captured me (Hannah seems to be a good name for a future president; there are several in the book)— not only with her picture, where she sits imposingly on her bike looking like she could take on anything, but with the words of this future diplomat: "If I became president there would be no wars. . . . There would be no guns of any sort. . . . Since we would be having no more war there would be a lot more money . . . we could give to charity. A lot of people need that money. Instead of killing people we would be helping people survive. A lot of people in Africa need it."

She's right, you know. Jeffrey Sachs, author of *The End of Poverty: Economic Possibilities for Our Time*, says you can follow the trail of war in Africa by following the poverty.

You can see how these outspoken young girls will grow up to be like the ambitious teenagers in this book, who intern for senators and congresswomen, join in civil rights marches, and volunteer for local charities. And it is clear that the teenagers will someday take paths as bold and diverse as the young women in these pages, from leading an Army unit and training female troops, to running for state legislature and lobbying Congress to reform the juvenile justice system.

Take Our Daughters to Work raised girls' aspirations, and we knew that their no-nonsense, justice-seeking voices would inspire adult women to reclaim their own courageous preadolescent selves. That's my hope for this book. I want mothers to buy the book for their daughters, though I think it will light a fire under mothers as well, inspiring them to run for school board or the state legislature. I hope fathers will buy it for their sons. After all, these girls and mothers are going to need smart guys in their lives and in their cabinets.

So thank you, Hillary and Shirley and Patricia and Elizabeth, for putting yourselves out there to lead. And thank you, Amy and Heather, for giving us the voices of another generation. We have no time to waste, because this time is ours.

MARIE C. WILSON
President and Founder,
The White House Project
February 2009

* 2007 Gallup poll: http://pewresearch.org/pubs/474/female-president

She's
OUT THERE!

★ ★ ★ ★ ★

INTRODUCTION

"**Where are all** the women?" asked nine-year-old Alexandra Desaulniers when visiting the White House portrait gallery. Her mother explained, "There are no portraits of women here because there haven't been any female presidents yet." That was the moment Alexandra decided she wanted the job. After hearing this story, I realized there must be a lot of young women out there thinking about running for president and wanted to know who they are!

What I found out is that Ms. Desaulniers is not alone. More and more American women are choosing to pursue careers in public service—and they are deciding to do so earlier and earlier in their lives. There may be disproportionately few high-profile female politicians in America today—but not for long. While women currently make up only 16 percent of governors, 17 percent of the House, and 16 percent of the Senate, women are starting to fill, in greater numbers, the ranks of local and state political offices. This seems only logical, since women make up 51 percent of the U.S. population. They are building a platform from which they will get to the higher positions.

And so, it is not a matter of *if* a woman will lead the United States, but a matter of *when*. Will it be in 2012? 2016? 2024? Who knows? But what we do know is that it is inevitable. *She is out there* somewhere—Who is she? What is she like?

To find out, I worked with the New York City–based research firm Fresh Perspectives and the nonprofit women's organization The White House Project to collect essays from young women nationwide who want to be president. My co-editor Heather Ogilvie and I chose the thirty-five best essays and traveled the country with award-winning photographer Robert A. Ripps to meet the young women. Robert took photos of the essayists in local settings that reflect their commitment to public service.

This collection of essays reveals what drives the political ambitions of a younger generation of American women, and it reveals their vision for our country. Between the ages of five and thirty-five, these outspoken girls and women represent our country's next generation of female political leaders. (We chose thirty-five essays because that number is also the minimum age for a United States president.)

The women in these pages are from twenty states and from diverse ethnic and socioeconomic backgrounds. They voice opinions from across the political spectrum. Two of the essayists—Agxibel Barajas and Jennifer Abraczinskas—are also featured in a 2008 documentary on women's leadership, *What's Your Point, Honey?* that I directed and produced with Susan Toffler. The film paints portraits of seven possible future presidential candidates at a pivotal moment in history, when the most viable female candidate ever was running for the highest office in the land. The movie shows that political equality is not about one breakthrough candidate; it is about hastening the day when just as many women grace the presidential debate podiums as men. On that day, the nation as a whole will, as Marie C. Wilson, founder and CEO of The White House Project says, "get beyond gender to agenda."

On page 203 I list thirty-five women currently serving in public office who have caught my eye as being potential future presidential candidates. I asked some of them what they would tell younger women considering a career in public service, and their words of advice are presented throughout the book.

Finally, in the back of the book, I list the women's groups and political organizations that can help young women who are interested in politics.

My hope is that the essays collected in this book will not only inspire other young women to speak out about issues that affect them and to pursue public office, but also give readers a sense of the direction female leadership is likely to take our country in the future. So take a look at these thirty-five young women—I think we'll be watching them for a long time.

—AMY SEWELL

35
EMERGING LEADERS

FIONA LOWENSTEIN

Age 13

New York, New York

Year eligible to run: 2032

Though I felt the outcome of the Bush-Gore election was very unfair, I doubt I would have become so interested in politics if things had not turned out the way they did.

LOWENSTEIN MEETS WITH REPRESENTATIVE CAROLYN MALONEY. SHE IS AN INTERN IN THE CONGRESSWOMAN'S NEW YORK CITY OFFICE.

I **sincerely hope** I am not the first woman president.

If by 2032, when I would be able to run for president, we still have not had a woman in the White House, then we are a disgrace. The other day, in my seventh grade social studies class, the teacher remarked about how far we have come with women in politics. I raised my hand and told him I disagreed completely. I told him I thought it was shameful that it is 2007 and the country still doubts a woman's ability to be its leader. It is an insult to me as a female that there are people in this country who would not even care what I might stand for, or could do for this country, and who would not vote for me simply because I am a woman. My teacher argued that that was my opinion, but when one looks at statistics and history, one can see it as fact.

I believe I have all the qualities necessary to become president, from leadership to compassion for others. I always strive to do the best I can and to help my friends or teammates do the same. I try to listen to people's concerns. When I am in a group, I am good at suggesting ideas and mediating. This is an important skill for a president to have, because the president needs to be able to find compromises and be willing to compromise. Compromise is key in making allies, and allies are key in leading a country.

Whenever I see a problem, I try my best to find a solution. I recognize world issues and try to help. When I was six, I began participating in the American Cancer Society's Dogswalk Against Cancer. In that first year,

I raised more than $500, which I donated to cancer research. I continued doing the walk for many years afterward. When I realize the importance of something and want to help, nothing can get in my way.

I am extremely outgoing and have an easy time speaking in front of people. The country needs a president who appears confident and isn't shy about meeting her constituents and listening to their concerns. Our citizens need a president who can appear dignified and represent our country when meeting with leaders of other countries. I could be that president.

I love to visit Washington, D.C. It's a great place with museums and sights, but my favorite thing to visit in Washington is the Capitol. It is a great sign of how open to the public our nation's government is. One can just stop in and voice a complaint—or compliment—to someone in Congress. The office doors are open, and receptionists and aides sit ready to help. Sometimes one can even speak to the congressperson him—or her!—self. When I first visited the Capitol, I went into Senator Hillary Clinton's office. Though she wasn't there, her staff was willing to speak to me and hear everything I had to say. I ended up having a really nice conversation, and they gave me their names and said if I am ever in Washington, D.C., again, they will try to help me meet Senator Clinton.

The first thing that really sparked my interest in politics was the George Bush vs. Al Gore election in 2000. During this time the news was always on in our house, and I heard lots of talk of the presidential race. I was only in first grade, but I wanted to know what was going on. As soon as my parents explained it to me, I was fascinated. Things happened that had never before happened in our history. Every morning after Election Day, I would ask my parents if anything had happened that might affect the result. Though I felt the outcome of the election was very unfair, I doubt I would have become so interested in politics if things had not turned out the way they did.

A few years later, when I was in fifth grade, my class participated in a mock debate of a bill. We dressed up as senators and went down to a courthouse in lower Manhattan. My teacher picked me as one of the leading senators; I was pro the bill. Up to this point, I had thought I might want to be a news reporter. But after debating the bill and finding a compromise, I decided that this was the best thing in the whole world. I knew then I wanted to go into politics.

A year later, when I was in sixth grade, our grade was to write independent research projects on any topic of our choice, as long as it was related to the theme "Taking a Stand: People, Events, and Ideas." Right away, I knew what I wanted my topic to be: Women in Politics. I wrote about the first women in American politics and present-day female senators and congresswomen. As part of my project, I wrote letters to women in Congress, and I was lucky enough to receive some replies. I spoke to staff from Speaker Nancy Pelosi and Representative Anna Eshoo's offices. I also got the opportunity to speak to Representative Carolyn Maloney of New York, Senator Lisa Murkowski of Alaska, Representative Barbara Lee of California, and former congresswoman and vice-presidential candidate Geraldine Ferraro. All of these women, both Democrats and Republicans, showed great leadership and patience. From speaking with them, I realize just how difficult a career in politics really is for a woman. In the end, I named my paper after something Speaker Pelosi had said: "There is a marble ceiling separating men from women in politics." I called my paper, *Breaking the Marble Ceiling: Women Who Led America.*

My research made me aware of just how few women there are in leadership positions in politics today. As of 2006, only 10 percent of the Senate and only 13 percent of the House of Representatives were female, while women make up more than half of the country. The road to political power, for women, has been very difficult. The first woman to run for president was Victoria Woodhull. When she announced her candidacy in 1870, women didn't even have the right to vote. When Woodhull lost the presidential election, she said, "The truth is I am too many years ahead of this age." Unfortunately, those words were still appropriate in 1984, when Representative Ferraro became the first woman to run for vice president on a major party ticket. So you can imagine how, when I saw Speaker Pelosi sitting next to Vice President Dick Cheney at the 2007 State of the Union address, I felt my heart swell. I felt the country had taken a big swing at the "marble ceiling," and really made a crack. A few more of those cracks and marble will be crashing down all over the country.

DID YOU KNOW?

- ⭐ **17 WOMEN**—13 Democrats and four Republicans—serve in the U.S. Senate.

- ⭐ **73 WOMEN**—56 Democrats and 17 Republicans—serve in the U.S. House of Representatives.

- ⭐ **SEVEN STATES**—Alaska, Connecticut, Hawaii, Kansas, Michigan, North Carolina, and Washington—have female governors.

Source: Center for American Women and Politics, Rutgers University; as of January 2009.

Many other countries have elected women as leaders, so it is surprising that America, a superpower, is so far behind. Why should Americans believe a woman would offer different leadership and guidance than a man? Imagine how many great presidents we might have missed out on, just because a small thing like gender got in the way. There may have been many women who could have been great presidents but did not run because they thought their gender was too big an obstacle. There are also women who did run but did not win because voters could not put aside their preconceived notions about women and vote for the best candidate.

Last year, my favorite TV show was *Commander In Chief*. Geena Davis played the nation's first woman president. The show made me wonder, "Was this the way our country would react to a woman president?" I believe this show might have actually helped the country get ready for a woman president. It showed the country a firm, strong, yet caring and humane female leader. Watching the show made me happy, but also impatient and frustrated. Even on the show, Madam President was appointed to the position, not elected. In fact, as of 2006, 56 of the 203 women who ever served in Congress were originally appointed to fill the seats of male senators and congressmen who were retiring or had passed away. That's more than 25 percent! This number is remarkable and depressing. Women are obviously capable leaders. We should be ready to vote for them.

The thought "Madam President" is constantly in my mind. I often try to push aside my doubts about our country's voters and have faith in their abilities to vote for a woman president. What I don't understand is how the country can look at all these wonderful, intelligent, passionate women who have done so well in politics, and still have trouble voting for a woman president. Maybe it's not that the country isn't ready for a woman president or that a woman isn't ready to be president; maybe it's that many voters are too stubborn and closed-minded to open their eyes and look at the facts. A woman is as good as a man. A woman is as smart as a man. A woman can be president.

If I were president, I would be able to lead our country through any difficult times or emergencies. I would resolve difficulties and help people and groups find compromises. I would raise awareness about various problems in the world and find ways to help. I would be proud to stand strong and confident when speaking to the country.

As I said, I don't want to be the first woman president. No, I have higher hopes than that. I want to be part of a long line of female presidents who have led this country with pride.

AGXIBEL BARAJAS

Age 22
Coachella, California
Year eligible to run: 2024

> *Few U.S.-born citizens would be willing to go through what undocumented residents go through to achieve a better life.*

BARAJAS, WHO'S APPLYING TO LAW SCHOOL, ADVOCATED FOR THE RIGHTS OF MIGRANT WORKERS WHO WORK IN THE FIELDS OF HER HOMETOWN.

Based on the course the Bush administration has led our country, I would have to be elected president and re-elected in order to set the country back on the right track. One term would not be enough to undo the damage that has been done to our nation and humanity overall. During my first term, I would introduce the appropriate policies. The second term would serve as follow-through, to make sure my policies were being implemented appropriately by people who don't put their self-interests first.

As president of the United States, I would put two items at the top of my agenda: public education and immigration.

PUBLIC EDUCATION. Mexican writer Carlos Fuentes said, "As we enter the twenty-first century one thing is clear: economic growth depends on quality of information and this, in turn, depends on quality of education." The quality of education in the United States is in great danger as the government continues to decrease the education budget. In 2006, Congress designated $56 billion to the education budget, a 1 percent reduction from 2005. Yet the 2007 military defense budget is $439.3 billion, more than seven times greater than the education budget. I would eliminate the major budget difference and allocate more money to education. It is not logical that education spending has taken a backseat to military spending. To ensure economic growth, our children must receive quality education.

Under our current system, only those from privileged backgrounds have access to quality education, while the underprivileged have to settle for a mediocre education. If we are all equal, as the Constitution states, then every student in this country should have an equal opportunity to get into college. To give each student that opportunity, I would reduce class sizes; provide each student with up-to-date textbooks, supplies, computers, Internet access, and tutors; hire highly qualified teachers; fire mediocre administrators and teachers; include a course of ethics in the high school curriculum; and foster a "going-to-college" attitude. I would raise teachers' salaries by 15 percent.

IMMIGRATION. First and foremost, I would discourage use of the term "illegal alien." I believe it is a racial slur that dehumanizes individuals. I would replace it with "undocumented resident." Furthermore, I would create a separate department for immigration and naturalization services outside of the Department of Homeland Security. Undocumented residents are not terrorists and should not be treated as such.

I would veto any bill that involved building a wall on the U.S.-Mexico border. Building a wall is a Third World solution to a First World problem. It is a waste of money and manpower. Regardless of the height and length of the wall, people would find a way of entering the United States. I would arrest the "patriotic" minutemen/vigilantes who are savagely killing human beings along the border. I would not send undocumented residents back to their native countries. Anyone who is willing to swim through a river full toxic waste and feces to escape hardship and oppression, anyone who walks across the desert without water for days in search of a better life, anyone who is willing to leave his loved ones behind so he can ultimately improve his family's life—anyone who goes through extraordinary means of entering the United States—is worthy of being an American. Not many U.S.-born citizens would be willing to go through what undocumented residents go through to achieve a better life.

I would take care of the undocumented residents already in the United States and address immigration from abroad. People leave their native countries because their governments cannot take care of them. As president, I would work with impoverished countries to improve the socioeconomic conditions that force people to leave their native countries. I would implement a system by which undocumented residents receive the rights and benefits that every individual who sets foot in the United States deserves. They would be required to go through a legalization process that would give them the tools necessary to become self-sufficient here, such as English-language and technical job skills. Furthermore, I would encourage immigrants to bring their families with them so that the money earned in the United States stays in the United States. Currently, undocumented residents wire millions of dollars a year to their families abroad. Thus, money earned in the United States is not spent in the United States and does not contribute to the economy.

Finally, I would educate Americans so that undocumented immigrants are not seen as a liability. They are the hardest working people I have ever met. The belief that they come to the United States to feed off the rest of us is a misconception. Undocumented residents who come here for the opportunity to work, earn money, and live free from the conditions they experienced in their homelands are not thieves or terrorists, nor are they lazy or stupid. They often take blue-collar jobs that middle-class Americans do not want, and provide services Americans take for granted. Yet, for all their hard work and sacrifice, they too often live in slums or tiny trailers, labor in fields in 100-plus degree weather, receive less than the minimum wage, have no access to health benefits, are discriminated against, and live every day in fear of being deported. Their situation should make every American ashamed for allowing this to happen on U.S. soil. We are too great a nation, too rich and too compassionate, not to make sure everyone lives with dignity.

I attended public schools in a low-income district all my life and was able to pursue a higher education at one of the best private institutions in the country. However, the shortcomings of my public education were evident when it came to competing with college students from privileged backgrounds. As a result, I had to work twice as hard to make up for the shortcomings of my education to be considered at least average.

As the daughter of immigrants, I am living proof that the stereotypes citizens hold against immigrants are just not true. Immigrants can come to the United States and become productive members of society.

My grandfather came to the United States in the mid-1940s and paved the way so that one day I could have a better life and the education he never had. I took it upon myself to accomplish his mission by seeking out opportunities and taking advantage of them to their full extent. Yet, my life does not end there. I am armed with a college degree and invaluable knowledge that I will use to encourage all people, particularly those with backgrounds similar to mine, to pursue their goals and dreams. As president of the United States, I would consider it my responsibility to give everyone an equal opportunity for success.

DID YOU KNOW?

- According to an analysis of exit polls by the Pew Hispanic Center, 9 percent of the electorate was Latino in 2008, up from 8 percent in 2004.

- The U.S. Department of Education received approximately 6 percent of the Fiscal Year 2008 U.S. budget. The U.S. Department of Defense received approximately 50 percent.

Source: www.gpoaccess.gov

KYERA SINGLETON

Age 17

Cherry Hill, New Jersey

Year eligible to run: 2028

"The country's leaders have invested so much money and time in the war that they have lost sight of the rising costs of college, as well as the declining standardized test scores of America's children."

My goal in life is to inspire, because without inspiration people lack the motivation to change the world. My endeavor to make a difference in my community, in individuals' lives, and in the world composes the essence of my being. Every aspect of my personality revolves around not only finding purpose in my life, but also inspiring others to do so as well. I thrive on the belief that hard work pays off in the end, no matter the gender or race of the individual. Therefore, I plan to overcome every racist and sexist stereotype so that one day I can make my mark as not only the first female president, but also the first African-American female president of the United States of America. My passion to make a difference is fueling my development into a powerful and influential leader.

My name is Kyera Singleton. When I was ten years old, I moved to Cherry Hill, New Jersey, from nearby Camden, once the most dangerous city in the country. While living in Camden I was encircled by people who believed they could never make anything out of themselves. Some died trying to find an escape from their lives through either the use or sale of drugs. Where education is the only major medium to securing a comfortable lifestyle, I witnessed the school system fail its residents. The poverty and desperation I saw led me to my love of politics. Through politics, laws can be made to benefit society as a whole, but more importantly, I can use politics to help secure a better life for all minorities.

Last summer, I interned with New Jersey State Senator John Adler.

Once a week, I went to Trenton with him for meetings on education reform. I watched senators discuss ways to improve the failing school system that many cities, such as Camden, experience. The meetings I observed truly inspired me. These men and women were working hard to ensure that every person had an equal opportunity to a great education. My internship meant the world to me, because I not only lived in Camden, but also attended public school there. Camden has

DID YOU KNOW?

⭐ The GI Bill of 1944 provided returning World War II veterans with college or vocational education, unemployment compensation, and low-cost loans for buying homes and starting businesses—though widespread racial discrimination at the time prevented many black veterans from ever receiving those benefits. The Post-9/11 GI Bill of 2008 provides educational benefits for veterans who have served in the military since 9/11.

⭐ The percentage of black students who did not complete high school decreased between 1990 and 2005, from 33.8 percent to 18.5 percent—which is still nearly double the percent of white students who did not complete high school (9.9 percent).

⭐ The 2005 unemployment rate for blacks who did not complete high school was 24 percent, compared to 11 percent for those who had completed high school and 4 percent for those with a bachelor's or higher degree.

Source: U.S. Department of Education Institute of Education Sciences, "Status and Trends in the Education of Racial and Ethnic Minorities," September 2007.

one of the worst school systems in the state of New Jersey. The education quality is far below that of its neighbor, Cherry Hill. There is no valid reason why one town's education should be superior to that of a town five minutes away. This summer, I volunteered ten hours a week, working without pay, in order to work with a senator who genuinely wants to fix the problems of public schools. My experience as an intern showed me that politics can result in positive changes for community problems. I have never wanted to do anything more than to help reform education and protect the students of the United States.

I feel that our past leaders have neglected many domestic issues, such as education reform. Since the GI Bill, education has been mishandled. Just as the GI Bill of 1944 denied African-American soldiers the free college education that it offered white soldiers, education is not properly reaching many minorities to this day. Many communities with large minority populations have failing school systems. The government is doing very little to fix this problem. The country's leaders have invested so much money and time in the war that they have lost sight of the rising costs of college, as well as the declining standardized test scores of America's children.

America needs an educated and motivated populace to contribute to the country's future success. If the children of America are not properly educated, they will never become leaders. Our past presidents have failed in the area of education reform; therefore, when I become president I will make sure that education is a priority. I will be the change I wish to see in the world. I wish to see every child in this country have access to a proper education, regardless of his or her socioeconomic class.

HILL CELEBRATES MEMORIAL DAY AT HER PARENTS' BACKYARD BARBEQUE.

LAUREN ELIZABETH HILL

Age 28

Massapequa Park, New York

Year eligible to run: 2016

I want young girls to know

that they are equal to men,

but more, I want them to

experience it.

Throughout our summer vacations, my cousin Jennifer and I would have sleepovers at my Great-Aunt Bobbie's house. Many times, Aunt Bobbie would welcome us to the kitchen table, where she had prepared a craft for us to do. Each afternoon, she would sit with us and discuss school and the beach. She'd talk about holiday plans and ask us what we wanted for Christmas, even though it was six months away. She was a dreamer, and her optimism was contagious.

One day, when we were not much older than eight, Aunt Bobbie asked my cousin and me what we wanted to do when we grew up. My cousin chirped, "I want to have a family and have six children!" Aunt Bobbie smiled, nodded her head, and said, "You'll make a lovely mother." They talked about babies until Jennifer asked to be excused to play with her dollhouse. I secretly loved it when Jennifer left, because it gave me more quiet time with Aunt Bobbie. I felt more comfortable to talk about my dreams when it was just the two of us. "Lauren," she'd say, not looking up from the yarn doll she was making, "what do *you* want to be?"

"President," I said, looking straight at her, expecting her to laugh, "of the United States." She stopped weaving, looked up, but didn't laugh. Not even a giggle. She smiled boldly and looked straight into my eyes, placing her hand on mine. "I hear children say things like that all the time," she said, squeezing my hand. "But when you say it, I believe you. I believe you *will* be president."

Her confidence in me was all it took for my dream to seem like a reality. And I've been chasing that dream ever since. After some time as a journalist, reporting on government and politics, and earning some awards in the process, I ventured into government. I worked in a State Assembly office for a bit and then spent a few years in town government, where I learned the basics of how government worked— or didn't in some cases. I then joined the region's largest civic and business organization in its government affairs department, and learned how to make friends with both sides of the political aisle, to create a better quality of life for residents through policy.

That brings us to what I'm up to now. I'm moving to Washington, D.C., to work on federal policy and lobbying on Capitol Hill on behalf of New York State. I'll be just a few blocks from the Capitol itself and a Metro stop away from The National Archives—I joke that I'm going to visit the Constitution on my lunch hour. But the best part of being there: I'm geographically closer to the White House and inches away from becoming a federal political player. Aunt Bobbie was long gone before the words "Madam Speaker" were uttered recently, but I'm sure she's watching, and I'm sure she's anticipating my introduction as "Ms. President."

Politics has affected my life in many ways—some positive, some less than positive. But despite the recent missteps of America's government, I have yet to lose faith in the system, and I know that I could make the system work the way the Founders intended. It is the democracy that exists in America that is so inspiring. We, the people, have the right and the responsibility to do what is best for the *common good*: for the good of the people we represent. The government created by our Constitution has the potential to be incredible and to return to what the framers of that great document had intended.

There needs to be a change. Special interest groups are ruling, and power is being pilfered. Right now America is ignoring its own residents and failing to take care of its most vulnerable citizens. In my opinion, the strength of a country can be measured by how it takes

care of its own sick, poor, and weak. We need to focus on those in need. Further, we're in a war without a strategy, without an end in sight. I had a loved one fight for his country this past year, and I know from first-hand experience what families are feeling: the uncertainty, frustration, and fear. But most of all, it's the politics being played with the lives of those we love that infuriates us the most.

The 2006 midterm elections exemplified how the forefathers envisioned a democracy working: Citizens dissented from the present administration using their most powerful tool—the vote. It was an incredible day for Americans; it reinforced the age-old ideal that their voices matter. It boosted my belief that I, one person, can make a difference.

I believe having a female president would demolish glass ceilings in every field, and empower women worldwide. I want young girls to know that they are equal to men, but more, I want them to experience it.

I won't say that I'm smarter than any president before me, but I will say that, if elected, I will make every effort to surround myself with people who are respected and knowledgeable—and, most important, I will listen to them. A good leader is strategic and practical, but a great leader is one who also dares to dream. I can be one of the great leaders.

DID YOU KNOW?

✪ The National Archives preserves and provides access to the vital records of the U.S. government. Here are some examples of the documents you can find there:

The Declaration of Independence

The U.S. Constitution

The Bill of Rights

The Emancipation Proclamation

The Nineteenth Amendment to the U.S. Constitution: Women's Right to Vote

The Voting Rights Act

Edison's Light Bulb Patent

The U.S. Supreme Court Decision in *Brown v. Board of Education*

The Apollo 11 Flight Plan

Elvis's Letter to President Nixon

HANNAH GEORGE

Age 10

Alameda, California

Year eligible to run: 2032

I think my ideas are good because they not only help the United States, they help the whole world.

GEORGE CAN OFTEN BE FOUND RIDING HER BIKE ALONG THE ALAMEDA WATERFRONT.

I feel I have great ideas. If I become president, there would be many things I could change. So here are my ideas written down.

If I become president, there would be no wars. The person I disagreed with would send a messenger to meet mine. They would meet somewhere special, like a restaurant or the Eiffel Tower. They would take notes of what the argument was about. Then they would go back to their presidents and say what they had written down. Next, the two messengers would meet again. They would say what the presidents thought about how to solve their disagreement. Then they would solve the problem. There would be no guns of any sort.

If I had been president over the past few years, the people in Iraq would not be dead. In wars everyone dies. I don't get that. Why don't we use words, the way we were taught in school? We were taught not to kick or hit people. We would tell them we disagreed or did not like something. We would not be like, "Hey, you're cheating on my math test," and kick him in the shins. You would tell him, in a nice way, to do his own test. I think that's how it should work.

Since we would be having no more wars, there would be a lot more money. With that money, we could give to charity. A lot of people need that money. Instead of killing people, we would be helping people survive. A lot of people in Africa need it. Kids are starving and dying there because they don't have enough money. It's really sad. I go to Berkeley, California, a lot and see people living in parks. Their beds will be a doorway or a bench. The most sacred thing to them is their sleeping bag or blanket. I've also been to Rome, Italy, and I saw homeless people with babies in their arms. The baby may never have an education or worse, just die. I think that is the saddest thing. Babies will be born into a family that can't support them. That's why we would give money. Think if you were starving to death. You know that feeling you get when you miss lunch. You feel sick. That's their day. They feel sick. That's why the money should go to them!

I also hate global warming! I think it is horrible. I think if the whole world worked together we could change global warming. We could raise the gas prices so everyone would get a bike, a biodiesel car, or an electric car. I think that would help. In my house we have special light bulbs. They save electricity. They will also last longer than other light bulbs, and they're brighter. I think everyone should get light bulbs like those. To help fight global warming you should not use your car as much. Ride a bike to the mall, or walk to the store. It not only gives you exercise, you are helping the Earth. A lot of people can walk to school and walk to the store. I think everyone should be doing it.

If I become president, on Saturdays, everyone in the neighborhood would gather together and pick up trash. Everyone would do it. People would clean their streets, sweep the sidewalk, and make sure the neighborhood looked clean. It would help everyone. They would have

DID YOU KNOW?

⊗ Madeleine Albright was the first woman to serve as U.S. Secretary of State. She was appointed by President Clinton and served from 1997 to 2001.

⊗ Over the course of a year, between 2.5 and 3.5 million people in America will live either on the streets or in an emergency shelter. Roughly a third of homeless adults are veterans. And 43 percent of children living with homeless parents are under the age of six. For ideas on what you can do to help the homeless, go to www.endhomelessness.org.

one day to vacuum and clean, wash their cars, and help their city. The world should not just *look* clean, but *be* clean. I mean, kids will stuff clothes under their beds. That is what I mean. The smoke from our cars mixes in with the air. It may look clean, but it is not.

All the bad troubles we have in our world would change if I was president. I think my ideas are good because they not only help the United States, they help the whole world. Everyone could take part in every one of these ideas. I think there is peace in the world, and I would like to expand it. I hope when I run for president you will vote for me. Thank you.

GOVERNOR
SARAH PALIN

🐘 (AK)

GET INVOLVED ON a grassroots level with an issue that you are passionate about and you can believe in. Totally ignore criticism that you can expect because of your age and gender—that's what I had to do! Accept as a young woman that you'll have to work harder—just accept that and deal with it. If not, don't even get involved in politics. Know what you're getting into and when you do get the resistance, just plow through it.

KARA ANN SILVERMAN

Age 24

New York, New York

Year eligible to run: 2020

"The petty, polarizing, political issues that have defined the last eight years in America have marginalized women's issues and threatened women's rights repeatedly."

SILVERMAN ANALYZES THE NEWS TICKERS IN TIMES SQUARE.

I am not a politician, I don't play games, and I am not interested in empty words and meaningless promises.

That being said, I want to be president of the United States. I have three reasons: First, I want a return to good government. Second, I want to reshape the image and role of the United States in the global community. Third, I want to represent women and women's issues in a way that has never been done by an elected official.

Throughout my life I have been politically active. Whether it was going to the polls with my mother as a two-year-old, running for office with my now-fiancé in college, or lobbying Congress on issues important to me, I have grown up believing in the power of our government to do good for the people. As Americans, we consider ourselves to be progressive, democratic people with a penchant for the free market and capitalism. Lately, however, nothing could be further from the truth. Our government has so corrupted its role in the lives of citizens that it is no longer effective. The petty, polarizing, political issues that have defined the last eight years in America have marginalized women's issues and threatened women's rights repeatedly. It is time to change the face of our leadership. It is time for women to stand up for what is important to us.

We are living in an historic and defining age for women and our country, and I cannot afford—no woman can afford—to let opportunities pass by.

America is in need of new ideas and a fresh direction. We need a government that is truly representative of the people, one that is as diverse and adaptable as the people it leads. We need a new vocabulary with which to discuss old issues; it is time to reintroduce words like *honesty, integrity, tenacity, fortitude, genuineness, thoughtfulness, respectfulness,* and *selflessness* into the American vernacular, and to create an environment conducive to change, growth, and maturity.

Right now our country has lost its identity, and we are struggling to get it back. Working in public affairs, media outreach, and communications—the "image industry"—has made me keenly aware of people's perceptions and the importance of having a genuine message. The president must be a good communicator; she helps to shape and express the national identity at home and abroad. The way the Bush administration was positioned, the misinformation we heard from it, and the way in which it communicated the president's decisions led to a dramatic downfall in support, both nationally and internationally, for the American government.

There are many voices contributing to the conversation about what it means to be an American, and not all of them are always heard. It can be easy for today's talking heads to ignore small nonprofits, community groups, or issue advocates lacking a large membership or deep pockets, in favor of bigger, established organizations. The president must be able to hear *all* of these voices, large and small, loud and soft, to govern the whole country, rather than be a representative of an elite class.

DID YOU KNOW?

⊛ In 2008, national ad spending by the Obama campaign was more than $310 million; the McCain campaign spent roughly $135 million.

⊛ In 2004, national ad spending by the Bush campaign was approximately $183 million; the Kerry campaign spent about $161 million.

Source: CNN.com; www.stateofthemedia.com.

We are a young country with a hopeful future that requires a leader who can temper the growing pains we face. Never before has America been so reviled in the global community; we must step back and reevaluate our position on foreign policy to ready ourselves to push forward with the confidence and conviction necessary to be a respected world leader once again. I think the key to a better, brighter, bolder America rests in our ability to embrace modernity, to move gracefully into the twenty-first century, to elect a woman as president of the United States. With a woman at the helm, government can be the vehicle for progress rather than an impediment.

As I look forward to what lies ahead for me and for my country, I believe that we are steadily approaching a crossroads where we can choose to rise to greatness or choose to continue down a destructive path. I hope one day to be the person who ushers America to the height of greatness I know we can achieve.

SENATOR
MARY LANDRIEU

(LA)

*S*INCE I ENTERED politics at the age of 23 in 1978, the numbers of women in the U.S. Senate and House have increased dramatically, and in state and local government, the numbers are even more dramatic. I could not be more proud of these accomplishments. Women bring a unique perspective to the integration of work, family, and neighborhood and a balance to the agenda that would be hard to accomplish in their absence. So believe in yourself, stay focused, and work hard.

ALEXANDRA ELISABETH DESAULNIERS

Age 18

Rockland, Maine

Year eligible to run: 2024

> *As a member of a small family aquaculture business, I have felt firsthand the impact of local, state, and federal policy on small business—the backbone of much of the nation's economy.*

DESAULNIERS HARVESTS OYSTERS AT HER FAMILY'S OYSTER FARM OFF THE COAST OF MAINE.

Since the age of nine I have known that I want to be president of the United States. During a tour of the White House, I gazed up in awe at each president's portrait. But I also wondered, "Where are all the women?" I was shocked when my mother told me that there had never been a woman president. And so my determination was sparked to become the very first.

My aspiration to serve in the Oval Office has never diminished over the years; in fact, it has grown as I have voraciously studied American and international government and policy in high school.

As a member of a small family aquaculture business in Maine, I have felt firsthand the impact of local, state, and federal policy on small business—the backbone of much of the nation's economy. While much of today's fiscal policy continues to stifle the creativity of entrepreneurship and drive upstart micro-businesses underground, the president has an ever-growing responsibility to work proactively to ensure that departments and agencies within federal and state governments develop policies that enable small businesses to succeed. Sound policies that would positively stimulate virtually every sector of the economy are already the primary focus of my presidential platform for 2024!

It has become painfully obvious that the status quo is not providing effective and dedicated solutions to meet the needs of America's citizens; nor is America providing adequate leadership for the free world. I understand that a president cannot afford the luxury of being a spectator to the games of foreign and domestic politics. She must be actively engaged in creating dynamic policies that enable our country to effectively and positively interact with our global partners. In the past, the United States has fallen victim to isolationist ideas. In the twenty-first century, we will need leaders who understand the increasing importance of networking domestically and globalizing internationally for not only the prosperity of the entire nation, but also for the benefit of other nations. She must understand and provide for the economic and social needs of America's citizens, whether they live and work in the big cities of California or in the agricultural hot spots of rural Kansas. I believe in these precepts and will, as president, someday make realities of opportunities for all Americans and forge positive partnerships internationally.

DID YOU KNOW?

⭐ Maine's Margaret Chase Smith was the first woman to be elected to both the U.S. House of Representatives and the U.S. Senate. At the 1964 Republican Convention, she became the first woman a major party named among its nominees for U.S. president.

⭐ Ten million U.S. businesses—or 40 percent of all privately held firms—are owned by women.

Now, as a senior in high school looking forward to a major in international comparative government at Colby College next fall, I have come to realize not only the great impact our president has on the United States, but also the great influence she may have on the rest of the world. I am also more convinced than ever that the United States is in dire need of a president who can deliver opportunities and results to her diverse constituencies. In the words of Margaret Chase Smith, a president must understand that "public service must be more than doing a job efficiently and honestly. It must be a complete dedication to the people and to the nation." In 2024, these are the principles I will embody as president of the United States.

RAY RUBIN

Age 22

San Francisco, California

Year eligible to run: 2024

"Our politicians are feeding us compromises in place of convictions, and we are eating it up."

RUBIN MEETS HER MOTHER—WHO IS NOW HER MOST ARDENT POLITICAL SUPPORTER—AT CITY LIGHTS BOOKSTORE IN SAN FRANCISCO.

Someone told me once that being president means you'll always be judged by the worst decision you ever made. The first thing I did when I heard that was scroll through my mind and rehash every bad decision to assess the potential harm it could do to my nonexistent campaign. I was seven.

I have always wanted to be president. I remember thoroughly embarrassing my parents (and myself, I suppose) with my standard answer to the "what do you want to be when you grow up" question. Some of the more doting adults would indulge me: "Oh, what would you change?" or "I'll vote for you!" But, for the most part, I got laughter and eye rolls to what I thought was a sincere answer to their question. By the time I was nine my mom had sat me down and explained that exclaiming such a lofty career goal was both immature and embarrassing. I tried to explain to her that my intentions were genuine. Then she laid it out very clearly. "You," she said, "will never be president, so cut it out."

Not that I could blame my mom. After all, she was a little skeptical of my platform. I was going to outlaw math and science, and make vegetables optional and chocolate required. I was going to force all the world's older brothers to go through sensitivity training and institute a national Kid's Day to make Mother's Day and Father's Day seem more fair.

Thirteen years later, I still want to be president, although my politics have transitioned a bit. I believe in all of the things you would expect from a twenty-two-year-old progressive: I believe in universal health care. I believe abortion should be legal and the death penalty should-n't. I believe we must make very concrete changes toward environ-mental sustainability. I believe war is never the answer, and the best way that we can help impoverished nations is with complete debt re-lief. And the less typically progressive beliefs: I believe in the abol-ishment of both marriage and the prison-industrial complex. I think this country owes people of African descent reparations. I think the government should pay for college for anyone who wants to go. And I do not believe a human being can be illegal. I also think we ought to send less money to Israel and spend more on creating real social change in the United States.

Unfortunately, these statements are not the ones that win elections. We like our candidates moderate and cautious—we don't want ex-tremes in politics. Just recently, *Time* magazine devoted its entire cover to that sentiment, stating, "Why the center is the new place to be," referring, of course, to the political middle ground that we're being told is the only place you can win. Our politicians are feeding us compromises in place of convictions, and we are eating it up.

But think back on the most significant social changes in this na-tion's history and imagine what the U.S. would look like if progressive politicians and civic leaders had been more concerned with winning their election than listening to their conscience. It was not compro-mise or middle ground that abolished slavery, or ensured women's right to vote, or led the civil rights movement. Those were radical, progressive choices that had to be made. Thankfully, we had leaders who made them.

I grew up in a family that valued community and social change. Both of my parents taught me, by example, that it was my responsi-bility to help leave the world a better place than I found it. So why would my decidedly independent, career-focused mother tell her only daughter that she would never be president? It could be that she just didn't think I was that smart or that her middle-class back-ground could have launched a presidency, or that my constant

DID YOU KNOW?

★ The Seneca Falls Convention, held on July 19 and 20, 1848, was the first women's rights convention in the United States. Organized by Elizabeth Cady Stanton and Lucretia Mott, the convention drew 300 people, including 40 men.

★ In 1994, the national children's crisis charity KidsPeace created National KidsDay as an annual event, typically held in August, to honor and celebrate the value of children and to encourage adults to spend more meaningful time with the nation's children.

tantrums weren't boding well for my war room sensibilities. But I think it was more likely a reflection of this country's general complacency with male leadership. As a nation, we have decided that we "aren't ready" to vote for a woman president and, for the most part, we're okay with it.

It would appear that our complacency with hypermasculine leadership is confined to the White House. After all, statistics show that we have made incredible strides to get women in positions of leadership everywhere else. We see women as CEOs, as doctors, as publishers, as lawyers, as newscasters, so it would appear that our (up till now) boys-only presidential hopefuls are not, in fact, a representation of society. But as long as it's men in the White House, women will be at the mercy of their decisions. I would like to instill in you a sense of urgency—we must focus our energies on getting a woman in the White House, and I'm certain, as certain as I was nineteen years ago, that I am the woman for the job.

Voting for such a progressive candidate will be scary; after all, a vote for me, a third-party candidate, is a vote for whatever fascist male Republican my opponent's opponent will turn out to be, right? Wrong. We must vote our hopes, not our fears. Many, many, many people in this country fought so hard so that we could have the right to vote, and we owe it to their legacy to vote for the candidate we believe in, not the major party candidate we think isn't "as bad as" the other major party candidate.

More than 150 years ago women organized the Seneca Falls Convention so that we could have the right to vote—that was the legacy they left. After that, women risked their lives to open the first abortion clinics—that was the legacy they left. Later on, women fought tooth and nail so that we could have equal footing in the boardroom, in the classroom, and on the sports fields—that was the legacy they left. This generation of women is going to vote into office the first female president—that is the legacy our generation will leave. So in 2024, when you see my name on the ballot and you ask yourself if we're "ready" for a progressive woman president, think about the legacy you want to leave for your daughters—and think very seriously about voting for me.

HASKINS REGISTERS PEOPLE TO VOTE AT THE INDIANA STATE FAIR, WHERE SHE
VOLUNTEERS IN THE INDIANA SECRETARY OF STATE'S BOOTH.

EMILY BROOKE HASKINS

Age 14

Greenwood, Indiana

Year eligible to run: 2028

When the Iroquois tribe made important decisions, they asked, "How will this affect the next seven generations?" I wonder what the world would be like if we did that today.

I can't remember a time when I didn't want to be president. I imagine it started around first grade. Kids look at you in shock when you announce your White House ambitions, right before they burst out laughing. But I just look them in the eye and laugh back!

Why do I want to be president? I'd love to say something noble like "Being president would put me in a position to end world hunger." But that wouldn't be honest. I want to be president because I'm fascinated by the way people use and respond to power (U.S. history is my favorite subject), and how their personal beliefs, no matter how hard they try to be impartial, influence their decisions. I want to be president because people say my gifts are the qualities of a natural leader. If I don't use those gifts in service, they're wasted. I want to be president because I don't understand how our current leaders can look at tragedies like the crisis in Sudan or in New Orleans after Hurricane Katrina, and not feel compelled to do something.

Last year, I was the new kid at Clark-Pleasant Intermediate, in Greenwood, Indiana; I recognized no one from my two months at the local elementary school. So I knew when I threw in my bid for student council president, I'd have to work hard. My mind flashed back to the previous fall when I had helped my mom on the campaign committee of a woman running for county clerk. Our chicken barbecues and similar events worked for her, so why not borrow some of those ideas?

My campaign slogan was "Em 4 Prez ... Now and Later"—now being student council in sixth grade, later being the Oval Office in 2028. I

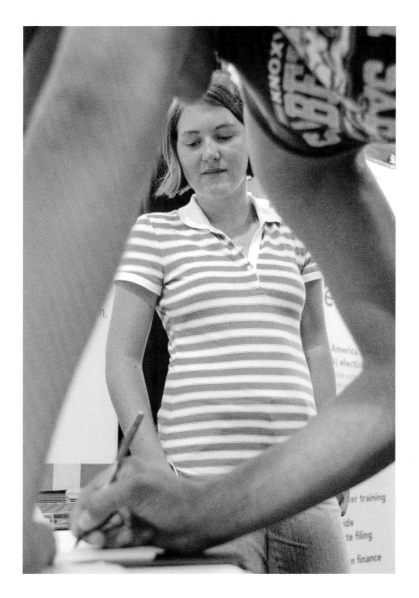

made posters, passed out "Now and Later" candies I had bought, and talked to people. When the day came to give speeches in front of the student body, I was shaking. But I learned something important that day: You never speak as horribly as you think you will, and most likely, people won't laugh, because they admire the fact that you can speak in front of a crowd. Being able to talk to people in a way that

Did You Know?

✪ Hurricane Katrina made landfall in Louisiana on August 29, 2005. As a Category 3 storm, with sustained winds of 125 m.p.h., Katrina was the sixth-strongest storm in U.S. history. Approximately 80 percent of New Orleans flooded, property damage exceeded $81.2 billion, and 1,836 people died, making Katrina one of the five deadliest storms in U.S. history.

✪ Since 2003, Sudanese government forces have fought rebel groups and waged a campaign of ethnic cleansing against civilians who are members of the same ethnic groups as the rebels. Hundreds of villages have been burned and destroyed, tens of thousands of civilians have died, and thousands of women and girls have been raped and assaulted. As of April 2008, some 2.5 million displaced people live in camps in Darfur, and more than 200,000 people have fled to neighboring Chad, where they live in refugee camps.

Source: Human Rights Watch, www.hrw.org.

stirs their emotions is key. I hope all of these lessons I learn in student government will give me a great political mind.

If I had to choose a political party today, I'd say I'm a moderate Republican. But both parties' beliefs and agendas are constantly changing, so I can't possibly say now what party I'll be representing when I run for president years from now. It may even be a new party. I think it's incredible that we have eighteen different kinds of Pepsi, but only two viable political parties.

When the Iroquois tribe made important decisions, they asked, "How will this affect the next seven generations?" I wonder what the world would be like if we did that today. When I am elected president, I will look after the interests of future generations as well as our own. The world today has complicated problems—we can't keep putting them off for our children to deal with.

I will be an honest president. There are so many dishonest politicians that politician jokes are as common as lawyer jokes. The people governing our country shouldn't be giving *Saturday Night Live* free material.

A woman president would bring a fresh perspective to the White House. We're not the girls of yesterday; we're not afraid to get our hands dirty. I'll balance grit and determination with empathy and patience. I'll follow the example of the eagle on our nation's seal: Always look toward peace, but resort to war if necessary.

It's a scary dream, to work hard so you can grow up to be the leader of the free world. The enormity of just saying that is overwhelming. But I feel I can earn my chance.

SHEPARD AND HER FELLOW ROTC CADETS TRAIN AT AN ARMY CAMP IN VIRGINIA.

MORGAN ASHLEY SHEPARD

Age 19

Upper Marlboro, Maryland

Year eligible to run: 2024

*Madam President. I was sure
that all of the work and
responsibility and criticism
were not for me.
Then I grew up.*

As a young girl I was always called "Madam President." I was the strong, intelligent, and serious girl. For a long time I hated my nickname because of its connotations. Madam President. How elitist and exclusive! I just wanted to be a normal girl, with normal friends and an ordinary life. I wanted boys to like me and talk to me, rather than fear me and slink away from me upon my entrance into a room. Madam President. I was sure that all of the work and responsibility and criticism were not for me.

Then I grew up. I graduated from high school and shed my identity as "Madam President" only to join the Army Reserve Officers' Training Corps and attend Georgetown University. My interest in government made declaring my major extremely easy, but I felt that something was missing in our university's government department—more women. So I turned to women's studies electives as a quick fix. I took a course entitled "Women in American Politics." I was astonished to learn that Professor Donna Brazile, the political strategist and former presidential campaign manager for Al Gore, would be my instructor for an entire semester.

Additionally, I found that being a cadet in ROTC taught me a lot about myself. At first, I was petrified at the idea of being an officer, a leader in the world's strongest army. Eventually though, I began to enjoy the nervous feeling that I got when leading a formation. And I was good at my job.

Academically, I still couldn't get enough of women's studies electives. So in the summer of 2006, I went to New York City to work for The

White House Project, a nonprofit organization that encourages women in leadership across all sectors of society. I had the time of my life working with women for women. Once back at Georgetown, a few friends and I created (or, technically, revived) the Georgetown University Women in Politics (WiP) group.

It wasn't until I was going through the process of restarting WiP that I realized how much of a lie I had been telling myself and everyone else. I was afraid to embrace the gift of leadership that I had been blessed with. I'd like to say that, as the president of the United States, my triumph will be the triumph of all women everywhere, but I am certain that there will be women who don't like me or who won't share my political views, and I accept that. I want to be the president of the United States because I enjoy being a leader. It is who I am. I like the feel of always strategizing to accomplish collective goals for others. I like thinking on my toes. I find that I work better when under pressure. I can take the criticism that may follow my actions.

As a student at Georgetown, politics has become a part of my everyday life. I find myself sharing educational venues with congressmen and women, diplomats, royalty, and other important political decision makers. It's amazing to be able to participate in protests for student aid and for Darfur all in the same week. As the president, I would be able to put so much of my current experiences to use. And I still have so much to learn. As a future officer, I face

DID YOU KNOW?

★ Donna Brazile is a political strategist, professor, author, and syndicated columnist. During Al Gore's 2000 presidential campaign, she became the first African American to manage a presidential campaign for a major party.

★ The Reserve Officers' Training Corp (ROTC) provides scholarships that allow young men and women to go to college while preparing to serve in the military after graduation.

lessons learned from the war in Iraq and from the current presidential administration.

I have yet to develop my brilliant, election-winning platform, but I am beginning to develop my own political identity. I have a passion for education, especially for improving our educational systems in low-income areas. I support social programs over the privatization of government. I am pro-choice, because I believe women have the right and the responsibility

to make decisions in the best interests of our health and that of our families. As the president, I will be sure not to fool the American people to accomplish personal goals, or to lie to, and jeopardize the integrity of, our nation, as our last two presidents have done. I hope that by the time I become president, more Americans will recognize and accept the challenge of becoming *world* citizens, so that we as a country can form a united front for international humanitarian rights.

I know now that the ordinary life I once wanted does not exist—and that even if it did, ordinary is not something to aspire to, but something to aspire beyond. That is why you'll see my name on the ballot in 2040, the year I plan to run. I'll be the extraordinary woman with big plans for an extraordinary nation.

RAQUEL RIVERA

Age 5

Imperial Beach, California

Year eligible to run: 2036

I don't want any more poor

persons. I want them to have

good lives, not bad lives.

RIVERA WALKS ALONG THE CALIFORNIA-MEXICO BORDER NEAR HER HOME.

I am Raquel Rivera. I am 5½ years old. My birthday is May 11. I have one brother and one sister. I speak English, and I speak Spanish. I was born in Chula Vista, California. I live in Imperial Beach, California.

I want to be president so I can let the persons of Mexico come here without a passport, even persons who are poor. And if persons have the job of driving those big vans taking persons back to Mexico [Border Patrol Agents], they will have to get another job.

I want more animals to live, maybe persons not eating so much meat. I don't want animals to lose their homes. More persons are taking their homes, the trees, and turning them into paper and not recycling it. Then squirrels and owls won't have homes.

I don't want any more poor persons. I want them to have good lives, not bad lives, and I want them to live very well.

DID YOU KNOW?

⊕ The official poverty rate in the U.S. in 2007 was 12.5 percent.

⊕ In 2007, 37.3 million people were living in poverty, up from 36.5 million in 2006.

⊕ Poverty rates in 2007 were statistically unchanged for non-Hispanic whites (8.2 percent), blacks (24.5 percent), and Asians (10.2 percent) from 2006. But the poverty rate increased for Hispanics (21.5 percent in 2007, up from 20.6 percent in 2006), as well as for children under 18 years old (18.0 percent in 2007, up from 17.4 percent in 2006).

Source: U.S. Census Bureau.

⊕ After a 2006 GAO Report entitled "Illegal Immigration: Border-Crossing Deaths Have Doubled Since 1995; Border Patrol's Efforts to Prevent Deaths Have Not Been Fully Evaluated," migrant deaths at the U.S.-Mexico border have decreased, from 463 in 2005 to 340 in 2007.

Source: www.lawg.org.

GRACE ANNE BALTICH

Age 30

Hanover, Minnesota

Year eligible to run: 2012

You can make only so much impact on public policy from the outside. The way to create the most change is to be on the inside of policy creation as an elected representative.

BALTICH CAMPAIGNS DOOR TO DOOR FOR A SEAT IN THE MINNESOTA HOUSE OF REPRESENTATIVES.

When **I was** six years old my father, who has multiple sclerosis, began using a wheelchair. I first became aware of politics and social justice as I watched my father struggle simply to gain access into buildings.

With my parents being political activists, I learned how building codes—laws created by politicians—allowed or disallowed access into buildings and indirectly restricted some individuals' ability to perform important life tasks. At my young age, I was impressed by my feminist mother's example of tireless advocacy for all forms of social justice. I vowed that I would change the world so that people like my father would not have to face avoidable oppressive circumstances.

I also vowed at that young age to change the world so that I, as a woman, would not have to experience being paid half the compensation of male coworkers for the same job or have to comply with dress codes forcing married women to wear skirts, as my mother had experienced.

At the age of seven, I distinctly recall being awed and empowered by Geraldine Ferraro running for vice president of the United States. I declared at that time that I would be the first woman president of the United States. But it was not until I was in my social work program in college that I took my declaration seriously. Now, with years of experience as a social worker, I have finally realized you can make only so much impact on public policy from the outside. The way to create the most change is to be on the inside of policy creation as an elected representative.

The passion burning inside me since I was a young girl now has a distinct goal: to become the president of the United States, to set the nation's agenda, and to lead this nation to equity and social justice in an inclusive manner. I have taken steps on my path to the White House: In 2008 I will run a second time for election to the Minnesota House of Representatives.

I have learned that, as a woman, I have a distinct ability to advocate for what is right and just, to work collaboratively, and to empower others. As a woman, I must do my part to move this nation forward, for my sisters and brothers, for my mother and father, for my children and their children—because who am I if I do not create the change that I seek and leave this world a more just place?

DID YOU KNOW?

- ✪ The Americans with Disabilities Act of 1990 (ADA), which was amended in 2008, prohibits discrimination based on an individual's disability. Other major federal laws protecting the rights of individuals with disabilities include the Fair Housing Act, the Architectural Barriers Act, and the Individuals with Disabilities Education Act.

- ✪ In 2007, the Equal Employment Opportunity Commission (EEOC) received 17,734 charges of disability discrimination. The EEOC resolved 15,708 disability discrimination charges in 2006 and recovered $54.4 million in monetary benefits for the aggrieved individuals.

GENEVIEVE GREENE FARLEY

Age 8

Tucson, Arizona

Year eligible to run: 2036

Global warming can be dangerous, and if we don't start doing something about it now, the children of today will be in trouble years from now.

FARLEY PERSUADED HER FATHER TO BUY A HYBRID CAR THAT WOULD MAKE A STRONG POLITICAL STATEMENT—EVEN WITHOUT THE BUMPER STICKERS.

My dad is an Arizona state senator. He inspired me to go into politics because he did things that were smart and right. I like that. He does things confidently—and I like confidence. My dad fights for transportation and has done good things. I want to stand up for good things for everyone.

When my dad was running for office, we walked in neighborhoods and knocked on doors together. I got him more than ten votes on my own. I love talking to people and telling them about my dad. One lady told me that she was voting for my dad because of what I had told her.

When I am president, I will address issues differently than our current leaders. For example, global warming can be dangerous, and if we don't start doing something about it now, the children of today will be in trouble years from now. Hurricanes and blizzards affect our lives, and global warming is causing more of them. I've seen the movie *An Inconvenient Truth*, which really woke me up to what could happen—we could all die.

I would shut down factories that make the most smoke. When I drive to Phoenix, there is a big factory along the road with lots of smoke. I would shut that down—and I have asked my dad to do that. We have a Prius car that runs on electricity and gas, and it is better for the environment than SUVs and Jeeps. My dad helped with a regional transportation plan that will help stop global warming. These are just a few things I think we need to do differently than our current leaders.

I want to be president of the United States because I feel there is a lot that needs to change. I believe I can make these changes because of my confidence and independence, and my ability to stand up for what is right.

Last week, for example, a boy (who had been a friend of mine) started playing a game he called "girl control," which meant he would chase me and push me against the fence and hold me there "until I died." I was strong, and I broke away. I talked with my mom about this, and we talked to the teacher, who made the boy write me an apology. He said he didn't understand that this was a big deal to me.

I believe it is important for leaders to stand up for what is right. I also think leaders need to understand that what might be a small deal to them is a big deal to other people. I can do this for our country, which is why I want to be president.

DID YOU KNOW?

★ Janet Napolitano, Arizona's third female governor, was the first woman to win reelection in that state. Before becoming governor, she was Arizona's first female attorney general. She is now the Secretary of Homeland Security.

★ According to the environmental watchdog group www.scorecard.com, the ten U.S. counties with the worst ratings on the air quality index are:

Imperial, CA

Inyo, CA

Mono, CA

Walla Walla, WA

El Paso, TX

Benton, WA

Dona Ana, NM

Anchorage, AK

Salt Lake, UT

San Diego, CA

WIETEKE ASTER HOLTHUIJZEN

Age 15

Boise, Idaho

Year eligible to run: 2028

" Growing up in conservative Idaho, I was often criticized, humiliated, and verbally harassed for my ideas and opinions. "

Holthuijzen takes a break in the Snake River Birds of Prey National Conservation Area near her home in Idaho.

If I were elected the first female president, it would be a monumental event in the history of this country. It would show that women can be president, even in the U.S.A., and would inspire, empower, and encourage women to pursue their dreams. Too often women are discouraged from reaching their goals, and with this victory, it would stop the prejudice and limitations that are aimed at women. We would finally be able to fully spread our wings, follow our ambitions, and prove to the world who we really are.

It was not until the sixth grade that I began to develop an interest in politics and see how it affects our day-to-day life. Every day, I listen to NPR in the morning and hear about the war in Iraq, for instance, or watch the news on TV and see the havoc of Hurricane Katrina. The effect of politics can be seen and felt everywhere. For example, my next-door neighbor left to fight in the Middle East, which really brought home the realization that we are a nation at war. All through middle school, I began to discover issues I felt strongly about, such as the environment and human rights. However, growing up in Idaho, I was often criticized, humiliated, and verbally harassed for my ideas and opinions, which were usually quite different from the conservative mainstream. At first, I felt hurt and depressed and did not want to participate in political discussions anymore, but as I became more engaged, I felt more and more compelled to speak out.

In high school, I joined the Student Civil Activists Club, a branch of Amnesty International. There I found students with similar views who wanted to make a difference and were willing to take a stand for their opinions. Together, we organized a protest at the Capitol in Boise against HJR 2, a bill proposing that marriage could only exist between a man and a woman. HJR 2 would have devastating effects, tearing apart families and denying rights to lesbian, gay, bisexual, transgender, and other unmarried couples and their families. We hoped that our protest would make some impact, yet the bill was still passed into law. Despite this defeat, I have decided not to remain silent anymore and to take a stand for what I feel strongly about. When I become president of the United States of America, I want to give all people a voice and a chance to express their opinions and ideas.

As president, I would place great emphasis on the environment. I became extremely frustrated when the U.S. government did not participate in the Kyoto Protocol. We cannot expect that there will be a never-ending supply of fossil fuels, and we cannot keep burning fossil fuels without worrying about damaging the atmosphere and our planet. That is downright ignorance; global warming will not go away by itself. It is said that ignorance is bliss, but ultimately ignorance may be responsible for the collapse of the planet if we do not take action now. As president, I would take steps to radically reduce the amount of greenhouse gases we release into the air. In addition, I would focus on conservation, sustainable living, and protecting forests, oceans, and other essential ecosystems, which are all crucial to stopping global warming. Also, I would start an educational campaign to inform and alert our nation about our environmental responsibilities toward the Earth.

Another issue I would concentrate on is the war on terror. Every day we hear of soldiers dying, car bombs exploding, and suicide bombers killing. Invading Iraq has been a disaster from the beginning, economically and in terms of the lives lost, for all of the men and women who have gone there and will never return, and for the citizens of Iraq and surrounding countries. Levels of violence have gone from bad to worse, and bombing is not solving anything. Musician and activist Michael

HOLTHUIJZEN HELPS
ELDERLY NEIGHBORS
WITH YARDWORK.

Franti once said, and it could not be truer, "We can bomb the world to pieces, but we can't bomb it into peace." We cannot expect to solve the problems in other countries' governments until we have fixed the problems within our own government.

As president, I would bring something special to the male-dominated government: a different perception of the world and a new, unique mindset. I have a strong vision for America, and when I am in a position to motivate the entire nation, I will be able to realize that vision. I see America becoming stronger economically, environmentally, and ethically. I see the people of America putting aside their petty differences, respecting each other, and living together peacefully. I want to work with people to help them solve problems of everyday life, such as environmental crises, poverty, and war. Once we have solved these problems, and have

DID YOU KNOW?

✪ Eleanor Roosevelt was First Lady of the United States from 1933 to 1945. One of the twentieth century's leading civil rights advocates, Roosevelt was appointed a U.S. Delegate to the United Nations, where she served as President and Chair of the U.N. Commission on Human Rights from 1947 to 1952. From 1961 to 1962, she served as Chair of the Presidential Commission on the Status of Women.

✪ The Kyoto Protocol is an international environmental treaty that establishes legally binding commitments for the reduction of six greenhouse gases produced by industrialized nations. As of 2008, 183 parties have ratified the protocol, which was initially adopted on December 11, 1997, in Kyoto, Japan, and which went into effect on February 16, 2005. Although a signatory to the Kyoto Protocol, the United States has neither ratified nor withdrawn from the protocol. The Kyoto Protocol is nonbinding on the United States unless ratified.

✪ According to the U.S. Energy Information Administration's most recent estimate in 2005, the United States is the largest per capita emitter of carbon dioxide from the burning of fossil fuels.

✪ Amnesty International is a worldwide organization of people who campaign for internationally recognized human rights for all. It has more than 2.2 million members and subscribers in more than 150 countries and regions. To learn more about Amnesty International, visit www.amnesty.org.

developed a sense of national unity and aid, we can move on to other troubled countries and extend our help there. I want to make this planet a better place for all, and I believe that I can best achieve this goal by becoming president of the United States of America.

Solving problems, whether political, social, or environmental, can sometimes look like a never-ending to-do list, and skeptics often believe it is impossible. Although it seems impossible to ever conquer poverty, overcome war, and restore peace, there is hope. As Eleanor Roosevelt said, "It isn't enough to talk about peace; one must believe in it. And it isn't enough to believe in it; one must work at it."

Often, the world looks like a cold, unchangeable place, and it seems as though one will never be able to make a difference. But with love, determination, hard work, and the help of many, we can change the world. Together, we can overcome hate, erode the barriers of prejudice, and end the reign of greed and corruption. Together, we can create a loving world, a place of equality and opportunity, with justice for all. Together, we can start to live within the boundaries of sustainability, not just for our sake or our children's sake, but for the sake of all life on our planet. I believe that this will be even more possible when I become president of the United States of America, and when we, as world citizens, pull together to make this planet a better place than we found it.

SECRETARY OF STATE
HILLARY RODHAM CLINTON

WHEN SOMEONE SAYS America can't elect a woman president, I say, come out on the campaign trail with me, see the mothers and fathers who lift their little girls onto their shoulders and whisper in their ears, 'See, you can be president, too.'

FOLASADE FAYEMI KAMMEN

Age 10

Oakland, California

Year eligible to run: 2032

" I am very sorry for the way

we have treated the planet,

and I want to help it. Too

many people and animals are

suffering for our mistakes. "

Kammen, a veteran of NASA Space Camp, tells visitors at Oakland's Chabot Observatory about the Rachel telescope.

The president of the United States of America is extremely important, not only for every American, but for every single person on Earth.

The United States of America has done and does many great things, but it is also the largest polluter on the planet. In fact, the U.S.A. produces 25 percent of the world's greenhouse gas emissions. We could, however, be doing a great deal to help clean up the world. As president, this would be my top priority.

Instead of polluting the world, the U.S.A. could help lead the world in an effort to stop pollution. We could do that by trying to convert as many gas stations as possible to clean ethanol stations. Hopefully, that would inspire many people to convert their cars to ethanol, or to make their next car a "flex-fuel" vehicle (one that can use gasoline or ethanol), and run it mainly on ethanol. That might also inspire other nations around the world to convert their own cars to ethanol. Ethanol is not the only solution; we could also use battery-powered cars, such as plug-in hybrid vehicles.

Recycling is also important. There is a new law stating that restaurants cannot use Styrofoam containers, which are made from petroleum. Now most businesses recycle, which is important because the United States produces so much garbage. This is a very good start to doing what we should always do, like trying to recycle as much as we can. The U.S.A. can lead the world by starting more recycling programs, and the president can lead the way.

Many animals are suffering for our environmental mistakes—for example, the warming we are now bringing to the planet. Polar bears are vanishing because the ice is not forming early in the winter, which means that the bears cannot hunt easily. In addition, the polar bears must go further out to hunt, where the ice is much less stable than before, so bears can fall through, become exhausted, and die.

The polar bear is not the only animal that is suffering from global warming. Birds are suffering more than we think. Because the world is heating a lot faster than we realize, during warmer winters birds perceive that spring has already come and lay their eggs early. The eggs will die because it will either be too cold or too warm for them to survive.

We are also already seeing changes in coral, such as bleaching due to the warmer waters, and slower growth because there is too much carbon in the ocean. Global warming affects coral by heating the water; when it gets too warm for the coral, it will turn brown and die. In Hawaii, there is some coral left, but it is all brown.

All around the world, not only animals but also people are suffering from global warming. For instance, many small islands, such as the Virgin Islands, will be partially under water within a few decades! The people who live there are starting to see a change. We need a leader who will make these problems clear and propose solutions.

Global warming is not the only issue where the president of the United States of America should lead. Another major issue is that health care is not as good in the U.S.A. as it could be. When I think about health care, I ask myself, "Is health care a privilege or a right?"

I believe that it is a right. I think the U.S. government should pay for people's flu, chicken pox, and other immunizations, as well as other health care. If we do not do this, those people who can't afford those types of shots and medicines will simply suffer. This is not acceptable, I believe. If a person needs something expensive like a kidney transplant, but can't afford it, the government should pay for the transplant and all of the expensive hospital bills.

DID YOU KNOW?

⭐ John Glenn, Jr., is a former astronaut who later had a prominent political career. Glenn was the first American to orbit the Earth, aboard the *Friendship 7* in 1962. After retiring from NASA, he served as a U.S. senator from 1974 to 1999. A Democrat, Glenn represented the state of Ohio. In 1998, Glenn became the oldest person to fly in space when, at age 77, he flew aboard the Space Shuttle *Discovery*.

⭐ Nearly 47 million Americans, or 16 percent of the population, did not have health insurance in 2005, the year for which the latest government data is available. The number of uninsured Americans has increased by almost 9 million since 2000.

⭐ The percentage of people (workers and dependents) with employment-based health insurance has dropped from 70 percent in 1987 to 59 percent in 2006. This is the lowest level of employment-based insurance coverage in more than a decade.

⭐ The number of uninsured children in 2006 was 8.7 million—or 11.7 percent of all children in the U.S.

Source: The National Coalition on Health Care, www.nchc.org.

If I were president, I would direct the nation to conserve our natural resources, and at the same time would urge the nation to develop clean energy systems. If I become the president of the U.S.A., I would do all I can to make the world a better place to live. I am very happy that people like Sir Richard Branson are taking a lead in environmental protection. This is something that the government could and should be doing. Sir Richard Branson is offering prizes to people who find a way to take greenhouse gases and other pollution out of the air. I think that it is a good start and we could be doing so much more.

I am very sorry for the way we have treated the planet, and I want to help it. Too many people and animals are suffering for our mistakes. If I were the president of the United States of America, I would try to change that. I would pass laws about preventing global warming and preserving nature. With any luck, the U.S.A. will "go green," and if we do, many other places will follow our model for development. The president must take the lead so that the United States can help itself, and at the same time help others. My goal is to be the best leader that the U.S. can have. I have confidence in the United States of America that we can do it!

INGRID SCHUSTER TIGHE

Age 31

Clifton Park, New York

Year eligible to run: 2012

I served in Baghdad, Iraq,

fighting the war on terrorism.

I saw firsthand the effects of

foreign policy implemented at

the lowest level—the

battlefield.

IN THE OFFICE OF HER NEW LEADERSHIP CONSULTING BUSINESS, TIGHE SURROUNDS HERSELF WITH HER ARMY MEMENTOS.

I **want to** be president of the United States one day to lead this country on a continued path of democracy where women, men, and children alike can continue to choose their destinies in life. My goal is to be a leader who influences other leaders in the world to accept democracy as their own and instill the values of freedom in their cultures. I hope to be regarded as a competent, intelligent, and passionate president who fights for what she believes in. My hope is that I will be viewed as the president of the United States, and not as "the female president of the United States." Through my example, I hope to prove to Americans and the rest of the world that women are great, capable, confident, and effective leaders.

With the awesome responsibility of the presidency, I wish to improve international relations with countries such as North Korea, Iran, and Venezuela. Relationships of trust and respect with these countries are necessary to promote safe and peaceful conditions for the future of America and the world. Moreover, my goal is to maintain our strong national defense and our premier military forces. While I hope not to have to exercise our military strength, I will be a leader who is capable of making tough decisions that ensure the safety of our citizens and democracy, if necessary. It is imperative to have a leader knowledgeable in military tactics and national defense, and my service in the Army gives me the foundation to make sound decisions in these areas. Additionally, I hope to improve education for Americans. Strong education

Did You Know?

⭐ In his 2002 State of the Union Address, President George W. Bush named Iran, Iraq, and North Korea as members of an "axis of evil." To justify a preemptive strike against such countries, President Bush accused axis of evil governments of seeking to develop weapons of mass destruction and aid terrorists.

⭐ Macedonia and Kosovo were once part of a country known as Yugoslavia. After World War II, Yugoslavia was made up of six socialist republics: Bosnia and Herzegovina, Croatia, Macedonia, Montenegro, Serbia (of which Kosovo was part), and Slovenia. In 1991, republics began seceding from Yugoslavia, sparking a series of wars. Within Serbia, government forces cracked down on Kosovars seeking independence. Huge numbers of refugees from Kosovo fled to Macedonia. In the late 1990s, NATO peacekeepers intervened in Kosovo and Macedonia to help stabilize the region and prevent the further persecution and killing of ethnic Albanian and non-Christian citizens.

⭐ The Republic of Kosovo declared itself an independent country in 2008, though not all members of the United Nations recognize it.

for our children will provide endless opportunities for them to pursue their hopes and dreams.

As a former soldier and captain in the United States Army, politics has affected my life very directly. During my military service, I deployed to Macedonia and Kosovo in 1999 as part of the NATO-U.S. peacekeeping mission. Additionally, I served in Baghdad, Iraq, fighting the war on terrorism. I saw firsthand the effects of foreign policy implemented at the lowest level—the battlefield. For instance, in Baghdad, my unit was charged with training Iraqi soldiers and Iraqi police to provide security for their country. Our progress toward success was, and still is, essential to our eventual withdrawal from the country. If the Iraqis cannot defend themselves and provide stability in Iraq, a possible civil war could result, which could have dire consequences for neighboring countries and fuel terrorist cells that we are trying so hard to dismantle. The pressure all of the way from Washington to the military is strong and affects all Americans, citizens and soldiers alike.

After returning from Iraq and separating from the U.S. Army in May 2005, I became involved in the local women's Republican group in Atlanta. I knew that I wanted to continue my work in public service, and I felt that through volunteer work I could keep abreast of local and state politics and make my voice heard. I participated in political events such as fundraisers for the governor of Georgia and for our local congressman. It was a tremendous way to get to know my locally elected officials and meet fellow supporters.

In April 2007, my family moved to New York, where I am now living in a suburb of Albany. In addition to volunteering for the local county Republican committee and preparing to run for public office, I am starting my own public speaking business aimed at young women. I will share my experiences as a female officer in Iraq to help other women learn leadership skills. During my deployment in Baghdad, I had the privilege of working with the first group of Iraqi female officers to join the Iraqi Army; I helped train and counsel them in leadership, decision making, and management skills to prepare them for their service to their country.

These same skills are important for our young American women to learn as they embark upon their own careers.

As president, I would work more closely with other countries in forming and implementing international policy. When several countries agree on policy and implement decisions together as allies, the message to the rest of the world is stronger and more effective. While I realize this may be easier said than done on certain issues, it is important to exhaust every means possible to come to consensus with other countries before acting on decisions alone. In the long run, without the support of our allies, the United States could become isolated. I am capable of cultivating close relationships built on trust, and I intend to use these skills in the international political arena. America is ready for a female president, and I am ready to take on the challenge.

GRIFFIN PRESENTS HER ANTILITTER PROPOSAL TO THE TUKWILA, WASHINGTON, CITY COUNCIL.

JACQUELINE OLIVIA GRIFFIN

Age 10

Tukwila, Washington

Year eligible to run: 2032

If I was president today, I

would try my hardest to stop

the Iraq war. I would work

with others to find a way to

solve problems without war.

I want to be president of the United States because there have been over forty men presidents since George Washington. I feel like it is time for change in the United States. There have been lots of women leaders in America, but none of them have reached the presidency. I feel that I could change America into one of the best places in the world. I know it would be a very hard job, but I would try my hardest to succeed. Like all things that are hard, when you're done, you feel very good, with a sense of accomplishment

A year ago, my mom ran for city council and won. I was able to help her with her campaign, and it taught me a lot. It taught me that if you care about the people in the city, you can do something about their problems by getting involved. My mom taught me that you can either sit and complain or find a way to help. That's what my mom did. I care about people in the United States, so a way to help them would be to be president.

Politics affects everything. It affects the roads we drive on, where I go to school, what food is in the local grocery store, gas prices, and what happens to my friends when their parents die. I have friends who lost both parents and their closest living relative is very far away and they only met him once. But the law says they have to go with this person even though there are people here who would take care of them. Through politics, a person could change that law.

If I was president today, I would try my hardest to stop the Iraq war. I would work with others to find a way to solve problems without war.

I have been a peer mediator at school, and we try to resolve each problem with steps to settle it. I think that something like that would work with countries at war.

As president, I would find a way for all Americans to have a roof over their heads, have enough food to eat, and feel safe. All kids would

GRIFFIN VOLUNTEERS AT HER LOCAL FIREHOUSE.

DID YOU KNOW?

⭐ Democrat Christine Gregoire is Washington's second female governor. She was elected in 2004 in the closest gubernatorial race in U.S. history.

⭐ Gregoire was reelected in 2008, with 53 percent of the vote.

get to go to school, and every adult who chooses to work would have a job. I would make sure all infants born here will be treated with respect and love as they grow.

I suppose the best way to start is to get involved in my city and state. I need to stay in school, get good grades, go to college, and succeed in life, so in 2032 I can run for president!

SENATOR
KAY BAILEY HUTCHISON

 (TX)

HISTORICALLY, WOMEN HAVE overcome the obstacles of being underappreciated and trivialized. We've had to work harder to prove our capabilities. I believe it's this spirit of perseverance that has propelled women to be so effective and that will continue to open doors to women at all levels of government.

ARENDT VOLUNTEERS AT A CHARITY AUCTION AT A CHURCH FAIR IN KENOSHA, WISCONSIN.

MEGAN ELIZABETH ARENDT

Age 18

Kenosha, Wisconsin

Year eligible to run: 2024

Learning about politics has made my life less self-centered and more focused on the world.

$\mathcal{A}$ll men and women *are* created equal, and I want to prove that by becoming an equally well-accomplished president as any man. My passion for politics has inspired me to examine current situations and to visualize possible improvements to revolutionize the executive office.

I want to run for president in 2040 to help the United States of America better focus on our future as an international superpower while also improving the quality of life for every American. Poverty is something that I would like to greatly reduce, if not eliminate. Our country has many more poor people than people who are well off. I want to change that.

I see international relations as the key to a strong future. Currently, the U.S. Department of State is working to promote a positive image of Americans abroad. Its efforts are useful, but I think that it is more effective to generate a positive opinion of America by helping other countries, rather than by staging pseudopositive publicity events or disseminating propaganda abroad. I want to work toward giving all countries a better understanding of our people, our government, and our culture.

My desire to learn through personal experiences will be a great attribute for a commander in chief. I will run for the presidency around the age of fifty so that I can learn more about the immense world before leading our country. To start my learning process, I intend to study and travel abroad extensively. I plan to spend time in the Peace Corps and would like to go through our Army's training camp to fully understand the basis of our nation's military. My first job goal is to be a Foreign Service officer—

DID YOU KNOW?

⭐ The Peace Corps was established in 1961 by President John F. Kennedy. Its goals are to help the people of foreign countries in meeting their need for trained men and women; to promote a better understanding of Americans on the part of the peoples served; and to promote a better understanding of other peoples on the part of Americans.

⭐ More than 190,000 volunteers and trainees have served in the Peace Corps to date, in 139 countries.

⭐ There are currently 8,079 Peace Corps volunteers and trainees, serving in 74 countries. Women make up 59 percent of Peace Corps volunteers.

⭐ The average age of a Peace Corps volunteer is 27; the oldest volunteer is 80.

which would allow me to more intimately learn about American national and international politics and the politics of countries where I would serve. I think that achieving these goals would lay the groundwork for me to be an excellent president.

Learning about politics has made my life less self-centered and more focused on the world. I first joined Model UN in high school because I had seen it portrayed in an Olsen twins movie and it looked intriguing. My first conference was an enlightening experience, opening my eyes to global issues to which, until that time, I had been completely oblivious: I represented Rwanda. After that conference, I became an intern for Russ Feingold's 2004 senatorial campaign and continued to become more interested in large issues affecting people other than just me. I have become more involved in my local community. And I love that the political organizations I have joined make sure I stay up to date on current issues around the nation and the world.

If elected president, I would never rush into a decision. I would be sure to have passionate spokespersons explain their sides of an issue to me before my advisors and I make a final decision. I want citizens to feel that they could come to me with their problems and trust that I would make the right decision, no matter what the circumstances were, because I would be better informed. I would be sure to stay aware of newly published books critiquing my administration so that I could seriously consider whether their suggestions would make a positive impact on our country.

Wanting to be the president is not enough; a person must gain as much knowledge and as many experiences as possible to lead her to that position. Our system of government is so complex; I would be completely dedicated to its continuous improvement. I would mend American relations with other nations while improving the lives of Americans at home. Politics is a great way to learn about the world, and it has shown me a side of the world of which I had not been aware, and now want to improve. I am confident that I will have the wisdom and judgment to ensure my success in office and the ability to maintain my "change the world" mentality.

REPRESENTATIVE
GRACE NAPOLITANO

 (CA)

OPPORTUNITIES AND GOALS that once seemed out of reach are now a reality for anyone who truly believes in herself. One person—one woman—truly can make a world of difference. Find your passion and trust your instincts.

NNOROMELE HANGS POSTERS DURING HER CAMPAIGN FOR STUDENT COUNCIL PRESIDENT AT HER MIDDLE SCHOOL.

CHIDINMA HANNAH NNOROMELE

Age 12

Richmond, Kentucky

Year eligible to run: 2032

As president you can easily reach out to help others—not only those who are like you, but even those who aren't like you. That's what I think presidents are there for— to help others.

My name is Chidinma Nnoromele, but I go by Hannah, my middle name. I'm twelve years old. I live in Richmond, Kentucky, and I go to a school on Eastern Kentucky University's campus, Model Laboratory School. There I am a seventh grade, middle school student. I am an African-American who loves being involved in many sports, including soccer, tennis, and track. I love to do all these things, but they are not my calling. I don't think that they are what I'm supposed to do in life for a career. I think my calling is to become a politician.

I started to grow interested in politics when I was a little kid. It all started when I watched the Al Gore and George Bush presidential election. As I watched the speeches, I would say with this sassy attitude, "I can do better than that. Let me show ya how it's done." Soon after, I wrote my own little speeches, pretending that I was running for president. My speeches included ideas such as "no more standardized tests in school" and "recess all day, every day." I was just doing it for fun. I wasn't looking at politics for a career. Then, in fourth grade, I decided to run for office in student council.

To be able to run for office in the Elementary Student Council, I first had to be a representative of my fourth grade homeroom class. I won that easily. It was almost unanimous that I be the class's girl representative. Then I decided to run for vice president. I ended up losing the race to my friend Ashley. I was heartbroken because I wanted to win so very badly. Even though I lost, I knew I would try again. I wanted to get as much experience as possible. While I was a representative, I studied and planned for ways to improve my strategies for upcoming elections.

In fifth grade, I was ready to run again, but we did not find a faculty member to sponsor the Elementary Student Council. I wanted to be in office so badly that I ran for fifth grade 4-H president. I won by many votes. This is when I knew I had the talent and the leadership qualities to actually be a politician in the future. I was hoping that when I got into middle school I would once again be seen as a leader.

Fortunately, I was. I ran for student council secretary of the whole middle school. Nobody really thought that I would win, because sixth graders do not get elected to the executive board. But I showed all my competitors that I had what it took to win. I came up with this catchy slogan, "Vote Hannah N. for student council secretary cuz yo momma would!!!" This got the crowd excited. It put most of the votes on my side. I didn't just want to win though. I wanted to change the middle school and make it better for all of us. At the moment, that's what I'm doing. With the help of the other student council members, we are making the middle school a safe and fun place to be around. I am glad to be achieving my goal.

Someday, I hope to become the president of the United States. I know this is my calling because I like to help people. As president you can easily reach out to the community and help others—not only those who are like you, but even those who aren't like you. That's what I think presidents are there for—to help others.

When I am elected president, a policy that I would keep almost the same is the No Child Left Behind Act. I like this policy because it challenges every child to reach his or her potential. I know that I'm not just going to school for the sake of going to school. I go to school to learn and be the best I can be. But I would change some parts of the policy, like how many tests each child would take a year. I would also change how schools are treated when they do not reach

DID YOU KNOW?

⊛ Marcus Garvey was a Jamaican-born social activist who encouraged blacks to take pride in their African ancestry and advocate for their rights. In 1914 he founded the Universal Negro Improvement Association.

⊛ The No Child Left Behind Act, or NCLB, is a federal law signed by President George W. Bush in 2002. Its goals are to increase the standards of accountability for states, school districts, and individual schools, and give parents greater choice over which schools their children attend.

the goal set by the government. Instead of making teachers reapply for their jobs, teachers will go through training that will help them find new teaching styles to put into place so that the children would learn more and reach the goal in the next year.

A policy that I would change almost completely is the environmental policy. Some of the acts President George W. Bush has put in place are not good for the environment. I do not agree with his stand on conservation and how he really didn't have many policies on keeping the water and the air clean. In my opinion, that's not cool, because we need these things for life.

I think that, with my strengths and my true desire to become president, I will succeed in winning the election and making America a better place. I want to become the first woman and the first African-American woman president. I know that if I keep my mind on the right path and if I study and try as hard as I can, anything is possible. The most important thing I think I need to succeed is confidence. My middle school principal, Ms. Skepple, always reminds me what the black nationalist leader Marcus Garvey said: "Without confidence you are twice defeated in the race of life; with confidence, you have won even before you have started." I know that I should keep this quote in my heart. And with my confidence, desire, and drive, I know that my future is bright. I also know that someday in the future you will address me as President Chidinma Hannah Nnoromele.

GREEN MEETS WITH FELLOW ATTENDEES OF A WOMEN'S LEADERSHIP CONFERENCE IN
NEW YORK CITY.

FARRAH GREEN

Age 24

Washington, D.C.

Year eligible to run: 2020

I learned that meeting with student leaders over coffee was more effective than planning programs.

By my junior year of college I thought I would be applying for the perfect summer internship to help me land a lucrative job after graduation. Instead, I was still trying to find the right major. I had started school as a confident business student hoping to become the CEO of a major corporation. I enjoyed my classes, but I soon realized that I needed more out of a career than money. I wanted to make a difference. I called it my "five-year-old dream" because I thought only five-year-olds still believed that they could save the world. Still, I had hope in Margaret Mead's famous quote: "Never doubt that a small group of thoughtful, committed citizens can change the world. Indeed, it's the only thing that ever has."

At the beginning of my junior year I sat next to Alison in one of my classes. I had met Alison only briefly freshman year, and though we had never really talked before, a familiar face is always nice in a big class-room. Before class started, we talked about our summer break. I had worked at Camp Judaea in North Carolina; she had interned at an Israel advocacy organization in Washington, D.C. The mutual connection was Israel, and she asked me to get involved on campus promoting the U.S.–Israel relationship. Before, supporting Israel meant attending programs with falafel and Israeli dancing or movies … and it was always the same students at each event. But working with Alison and two others, I helped register over 250 pro-Israel students to vote, organize presidential debate-watching parties with the College Democrats and College Republicans, and build relationships with our elected officials.

And I learned my first political lesson: that meeting with student leaders over coffee was more effective than planning programs. Individual meetings turned into long-lasting friendships, and we worked together to help advance each other's causes. I finally felt as though I was making a difference. The leadership and political skills that I learned from Alison through the lens of Israel could be applied to any issue. Until then, senators and representatives were "fairy tale" people in offices far, far away. With Alison's help, I became comfortable calling those offices to schedule meetings with members of Congress. Moreover, I was able to empower others to do the same.

I learned that to really make a difference, voting is not enough. By the time one casts her vote, most of the decisions have already been made. Too often, Americans feel they are forced to vote between the lesser of two evils. This is the problem; spectacular citizenship is the solution.

Our government was created to be representative of its people. This works only when citizens get involved in the process. Volunteering on campaigns, lobbying elected officials, and serving in public office are not only our right, but our responsibility. Too many people believe in the bleak fairy tale of out-of-touch members of Congress and helpless citizens.

The leaders of America need to lead, engage, and listen to their constituents year round, not only during elections. Additionally, America needs to look to other nations and learn from their successes and failures. America's strength cannot be taken for granted. As president, I would use the first political lesson I learned to build relationships, partnerships, and friendships with nations abroad to help advance America's interests and to foster a global community in which nations care about one other and work together to solve problems. At home, I would work to build relationships and form coalitions with elected officials on both sides of the aisle.

My life is forever changed because one person asked me to get involved. Now I am working to engage and empower others to do

DID YOU KNOW?

★ Margaret Mead was a cultural anthropologist who wrote many bestselling books, including *Coming of Age in Samoa* (1928). A large part of her work focused on gender roles not only in primitive societies but also in contemporary American culture.

the same so that they can work to advance the issues they believe in. I hope to continue to empower individuals and strengthen communities by running for and serving in public office. For community, access, and leadership, vote Farrah Green for president in 2036!

REPRESENTATIVE
LORETTA SANCHEZ

(CA)

on't be discouraged if you don't fit an established sense of how a leader is supposed to look or sound. In my first term I got stopped by police all the time when going into the Capitol because I didn't fit their preconceived notion of what a Member of Congress looks like. You need to blaze your own path and set your own example rather than be defined by someone else's—otherwise change will never come.

KOSSEK AND FELLOW STUDENTS ATTENDING A SUMMER PROGRAM FOR GIFTED YOUTH
PAINT A ROCK ON THE UNIVERSITY OF MICHIGAN CAMPUS TO PUBLICIZE "1 OF 6 DAY,"
A POVERTY-AWARENESS EVENT TO RAISE MONEY FOR UNICEF, ACTION AGAINST
HUNGER, AND THE INVISIBLE CHILDREN.

HALEY ROBINSON KOSSEK

Age 16

Williamsburg, Michigan

Year eligible to run: 2028

I want to be president because

I'm a girl with opinions.

I want to be heard, and I

want the echo to be loud.

As a sixteen-year-old feminist blog junkie who asks for copies of *Gender Outlaw* and *This Bridge Called My Back* as birthday presents, I have been passionate about politics ever since elementary school, when I was one of the only girls in an advanced math group and would always choose the Seneca Falls Convention as a topic for history reports.

Being a teenage social justice advocate, especially in my small-town, rural environment, means a lot of things. It means being that kid who always raises her hand in class to point out something as ethnocentric or heteronormative. It means awkward looks, from both classmates and teachers, when walking into class wearing a THIS IS WHAT A FEMINIST LOOKS LIKE T-shirt. It means whispers in the hallways and graffiti in bathroom stalls: "That girl's a dyke."

But it also means having an understanding, an awareness, and a passion about something more substantial than the *American Idol* results. It means having a purpose and a message. No matter how often the mainstream culture tells me that's wrong—that I, as a girl, especially a teenage girl, shouldn't have opinions—I refuse to let it silence me. Call me what you will; I'll still believe that equality and justice are worth fighting for.

I want to be president because I'm a girl with opinions. I want to be heard, and I want the echo to be *loud*. The United States presidency, maybe above all of the other roles it fulfills, is the world's biggest soapbox. A single speech by the president makes headline news; historically, by actively discussing and promoting certain issues, presidents have permanently altered the political landscape.

Hear me? That girl protesting outside your window? Shouting through her keyboard as she blogs about her latest encounter with something she just refuses to accept? Beliefs, needs, demands—mine and other women's—I want them to be *heard*. Women have long been told that individual thought was wrong. Look at the glossy magazines in the grocery store check-out line. Observe the dearth of female columnists and pundits. The message is: Girls don't advocate—at least, they shouldn't (especially not girls of color, girls with disabilities, and low-income girls). If they do stand up for their opinions, they're aggressive, ballbusters, manhaters, dirty. They should shut up.

Anna Quindlen, the third woman ever to write for *The New York Times* Op-Ed page, began one of her books of Pulitzer Prize-winning columns with the line, "These are my words; this is their world, a world in which we can wear our gender on our sleeves, unabashedly, as we go about the business of

DID YOU KNOW?

⊛ Barbara Smith is the black feminist who coined the term "identity politics." She has been a writer and lecturer on black feminism and has recently served on the Albany, N.Y., city council.

⊛ Published in 1994, *Gender Outlaw* was written by Kate Bornstein, a lesbian who was formerly a heterosexual male, about the role of gender and identity in our culture and in her own transgender experience.

⊛ First published in 1981, *This Bridge Called My Back: Writings by Radical Women of Color* is an influential collection of feminist essays, edited by Cherrie Moraga and Gloria E. Anzaldua.

thinking out loud." As I pursue my goals, thanks to the work of such leaders as Quindlen, I will be able to wear my gender on my sleeve, unabashedly, as I go about the business of thinking out loud. So I might as well take those thoughts to where they will be heard the loudest.

Barbara Smith, an influential feminist of color, said that any true feminist movement must inherently also fight racism, ableism, class inequality—if the movement doesn't represent the needs of *all* women, including those in specifically disadvantaged groups, then it "is not feminism, but merely female self-aggrandizement."

In working to express this viewpoint through the presidency, I hope to represent those whose needs and opinions are often left out of the policymaking discussions in Washington. I will speak for the needs of *all* disadvantaged people, and in doing so, start a lasting conversation on social justice in America.

REPRESENTATIVE
DEBBIE WASSERMAN SCHULTZ

 (FL)

WE WOMEN ALWAYS want to do it all. Stop wondering how you're going to fit it all in, and just move forward. Follow your passion, embrace imperfection, run for office, ask for help when you need it, and you'll find a way to make it work.

JENNIFER LOUISE SEARFOSS

Age 30

Ada, Michigan

Year eligible to run: 2012

Politics is a hands-on activity. I have no interest in being a backroom idea person; instead, I invest considerable time and resources in engaging voters.

VOLUNTEERING FOR ADOPT-A-HIGHWAY, SEARFOSS PICKS UP TRASH ALONG A STRETCH OF HIGHWAY OUTSIDE ANNAPOLIS, MARYLAND.

The president of the United States can and should be the most influential figure in the world. Her actions impact the health and well-being of the globe; and thus, I believe that the faithful execution of this office is the most solemn duty to be bestowed on a U.S. citizen. The president must possess not only the courage and passion to inspire our nation to grow, but also the compassion to comfort the American public in our times of trial. Ultimately, the president should be the embodiment of the ideals of our people and inspire hope for the country's future.

Presidents Franklin Delano Roosevelt and John F. Kennedy set the standard for leadership that has been lacking during my lifetime. These leaders inspire my vision of the American presidency, which is to preserve the sanctity of the Constitution, promote the freedoms uniquely afforded to Americans, and rebuild the global image of our country. Great leaders must strive to promote these principles. I believe I can be that next great leader. It is for this reason that I welcome the opportunity to proudly serve as commander in chief.

Politics is a hands-on activity. I have no interest in being a backroom idea person; instead, I invest considerable time and resources in engaging voters. I acknowledge that politics touches every aspect of my life: from where my father was stationed in the U.S. Army, moving us across the nation; to how much I repay on student loans each month; to how fast I drive. The political process has created the reality of the American lifestyle.

DID YOU KNOW?

⊛ Alice Paul was one of the leading suffragists responsible for the passage of the Nineteenth Amendment to the U.S. Constitution, which gave women the right to vote. Later in her long life (1885–1977) she was also instrumental in creating and campaigning for the Equal Rights Amendment.

⊛ Susan B. Anthony was a prominent civil rights leader in the 1800s, advocating for the voting rights of blacks and women. In 1869, Anthony and Elizabeth Cady Stanton founded the National Women's Suffrage Association. Anthony died in 1906, 14 years before women got the right to vote.

It is for this reason that I have put my feet to the pavement, listened to voters and the disenfranchised to better understand their daily concerns, and appreciated how the political process can and will define their livelihoods. In 2006, I saw my name on the ballot for the first time when I ran in a district-wide race for the county political central committee. Although a party election, my race was highly controversial, since I did not ask the local political machine for endorsement or approval of my run for the seat. As an outsider, I was openly threatened and was told I would be "crushed." Vandalism, rumors, and dirty politics did not stop me. I knocked on many doors in my district and ran an old-fashioned campaign, meeting voters and talking about the lack of party infrastructure that the establishment promoted and sought to preserve. The voters listened, and I was rewarded with not only the highest vote count for the position in the district, but also the second-highest in the county. It was a humbling experience and one that I shall never forget.

I have made it my life's work to be a political advocate. In this role, I seek out solutions to problems and actively push for resolution through consensus building. Coming from a long line of medical professionals, I have continued the family tradition and studied to become a health care attorney. Thus, the political process has greatly affected my life and how I lead it. I work to ensure that every person I represent has his or her voice heard in the decision-making process at all levels of government.

Yet, I find that as a woman, I am faced with incredibly different hurdles from the ones my male counterparts face. The roles of caretaker, wife, and mother are social pressures that are not easily incorporated into my busy career. It is for this reason that I recently chose to resign my seat, leave my Maryland home of ten years, and relocate to Michigan to take care of my mother who is learning to walk and be independent again after three life-changing surgeries.

Despite this new challenge, my passion for politics is not diluted by my personal struggles. I hope to learn from women who have successfully made their marriages work and find personal fulfillment in career, family, and politics. It is a delicate balance that I will strive to achieve over the course of my lifetime. I continue to work on improving the world around me and find no need to look beyond the past six years to identify what I, as president, would do differently. Specifically, three sacred values and principles would define my presidency:

1. Liberty: I will uphold our Constitution and defend civil liberties.
2. Honesty: The American people deserve the truth. I will publicly explain my actions and take responsibilities for the decisions I make.
3. Community: I will work for the betterment of all Americans, and not merely for a few special interests.

My generation did not march for the Equal Rights Amendment and largely does not appreciate the political battles that Susan B. Anthony and Alice Paul fought so that all women could be part of the political process. However, their legacy and the legacies of many other leaders inspire me to enact change to improve the lives of *all* Americans. Instead of waiting for the next leader, I choose to step forward and serve.

HALEY PREININGER

Age 11

Bradenton, Florida

Year eligible to run: 2032

If we do not have strong security there might be more terrorist attacks, and our country could be in danger.

My name is Haley, and I am an eleven-year-old Republican hoping to become the first woman president of the United States. I am currently in sixth grade at the Out-of-Door Academy. First, I would make a great president because I am aware of the problems currently going on in our country. Second, I am a great and smart leader. Last, I am very organized and conscientious.

I am aware of the current problems of the United States, such as fighting the war in Iraq, finding Osama bin Laden, and maintaining homeland security. For the war in Iraq, I would have a well-thought-out plan so our troops can go in and out, accomplishing what they went there to do. Finding Osama bin Laden is important because he is the one responsible for attacking the World Trade Center and killing thousands. To find him, I would search in other surrounding countries such as Turkey, Saudi Arabia, and Syria. Last, but not least, maintaining homeland security: If we do not have strong security there might be more terrorist attacks, and our country could be in danger. I think we should have more homeland security around popular areas such as New York City and Washington, D.C., because with the war going on in Iraq, a terrorist might try to come here with dangerous weapons.

Being a great leader is a good quality for a president because you are representing and leading the entire country. The president must lead *everyone*. Being smart is also a good quality because you can make better and quicker choices.

Last, I am very organized and conscientious. Being organized is very important because if you lose one paper the whole country could suffer. I am personally very organized because I'm always on top of all of my school assignments and never turn in anything late. When I hear about a new project, I always start it early to make sure it is perfect when I turn it in. Also, once I hear about an extra task or assignment, my new goal is to complete it. Being conscientious is a good quality because if you are not dedicated to your work, and slack off, people would start to feel that no one is leading our country, and it would slowly fall apart.

I am very capable of being the first—or next—female president because I am aware of the problems currently going on in our country, I am a very great and smart leader, and I am very organized and conscientious. I hope you agree with me and believe that I am up to the challenge.

DID YOU KNOW?

⭐ World Trade Center facts:

GROUNDBREAKING: 8/5/66

RIBBON-CUTTING: 4/4/73

HEIGHT: 1,368 feet and 1,362 feet, respectively (tallest buildings in the world until the Sears Tower was built in 1974)

OCCUPANTS: 430 businesses from 26 countries; 50,000 people worked in the Towers

DESTROYED: 9/11/01

FATALITIES ON 9/11/01: 2,604, plus 146 on the planes that hit the Towers (and 24 people are still listed as missing)

⭐ The Department of Homeland Security (DHS) was created on November 25, 2002, in response to the terrorist attacks of September 11, 2001. The third-largest cabinet department, DHS is charged with protecting the United States from terrorist attacks and responding to natural disasters.

ELIZABETH MCINTOSH

Age 16

Bend, Oregon

Year eligible to run: 2028

It may be cliché to say: "I want to make the world a better place." But isn't that what we all want?

MCINTOSH BELIEVES THAT COMMITMENT TO THE ENVIRONMENT, LIKE STUDYING BALLET, TAKES DISCIPLINE. WITH THE HELP OF THESE BACKYARD SOLAR PANELS AND A WIND GENERATOR, HER HOUSE IS ENERGY-INDEPENDENT.

Why do I want to be president? It's a compulsion to do something better for my family and friends, my country, and ultimately the world. I want to be president because when I watch the news or read the newspaper I am often sickened by what I see. I see the world we all cherish being lost to terror and violence, a world becoming immune to the suffering in the Middle East and Darfur. I am scared that we as a nation—and as individuals—can watch the news footage of bombs exploding and people dying and not give these events a second thought, but continue eating our dinner or doing our homework.

In the fourth grade, when a former female speaker of the Oregon House of Representatives came to visit my class and we held a mock congress, I decided that I liked politics. It seemed so simple in those days to make a difference.

Well, now I am older. I have lived through the now infamous Bush v. Gore election, felt the national tragedy of 9/11, watched my country go into two wars that have not ended, and seen the casualty list grow longer and longer, with no hope for it to slacken its pace. My fervor to change things has only increased with these events. So that is why I want to be president. Every time I watch the news, or discuss current events in history class, I am driven to try to change things. It may be cliché to say: "I want to make the world a better place." But isn't that what we all want?

The word "politics" may strike hate in the heart of many Americans, but me, I love politics. Politics has taught me that there is always a way to change things.

For example, my town has refused for 10 years to build a new high school; the current one was built in the 1970s to serve about 1,200 students and now serves 1,800. So the school board decided to convert

an old middle school into an annex and to house the new "smaller learning communities" (SLCs)—including the International Baccalaureate program I am attending—in the annex. But then, about six weeks into the school year, the board decided that not enough students were attending the smaller programs and the building would be converted into a freshman campus. I was appalled! How could they do this only six weeks into the year, when new programs always take time? So I thought about politics and decided that I had to do something. I had to show the board why it was in their best interest to keep the SLCs at that building. I spoke at a school board meeting. And the next day the superintendent was in our classroom. And a week later a large public forum was scheduled to discuss the issue. Politics showed me that sometimes all it takes is a speech and some persuasion to get what you want: The SLCs stayed at the old middle school building, and enrollment is projected to increase greatly next year.

I would like to say that I would be the one president who would be different, who could change the world, and who would be an independent leader. But I know that is naïve and idealistic. So I have decided to settle for more realistic goals: to fix the national health care problem by providing the uninsured with government health insurance, but also allowing private insurance. I wish to tame the drug epidemic by providing homes for the homeless so that fewer people end up on the streets selling drugs to survive. I wish to focus on the domestic issues, because our country cannot help others when we do not function ourselves. But not to neglect the rest of the world, I wish to help reform the United Nations and limit the powers of the five permanent member-countries of the Security Council. I want to help advance the status of women in the Middle East and end genocide in the world. I will use diplomacy rather than force and extend a hand of friendship so that conflicts will become few and hopefully far between.

My goals as president seem to reflect common ideas and promises made by politicians. But so often the promises that win a campaign take a backseat once the presidency is won. When I become president, I will take a stand and fight for the common good of our nation so that our country can see what good can come of politics, rather than just the negative.

AT A FAMILY REUNION OUTSIDE KALAMAZOO, MICHIGAN, ULMER IS SURROUNDED BY
FRIENDS AND SEVERAL GENERATIONS OF FAMILY MEMBERS.

CORINA ULMER

Age 22

Kalamazoo, Michigan

Year eligible to run: 2020

The Bush administration has put too much emphasis on foreign affairs and global power, and not enough on domestic needs and reform at fundamental levels.

In decades past, to toy with the notion of a female president would not only have been taboo, but comical. At one point in American history, women were not even allowed to ride bicycles, let alone be in charge of the most powerful nation in the world. But today, we are closer than ever before to hearing the two wonderful words: "Madam President." I'm not sure if it is the power of being a "Third Wave" feminist, the excitement surrounding Senator Clinton, or the result of growing up with good old girl power, but when people ask me what I want to do with my life, I no longer say, "Be a television journalist." What comes out of my mouth is, "Be the president of the United States."

Because I'm a woman, politics affects every day of my life, from the politicalization of my education and salary to the politicalization of my body and health care. I have chosen to define myself on many levels through politics. Living an activist life, I am continually standing up for my political and social values and beliefs. After becoming very involved in Third Wave feminism in college, I became aware of the political oppressions forced upon my fellow students and me. Not only do women lack sufficient representation in higher education, but we are also constantly held to double standards in many areas of our lives. The constant struggles to eradicate violence against women seem like muffled cries in our desensitized society. And many still argue against the fact that women's rights are human rights. Faced with that, I no longer think politics is something complicated, but something I know I need to change.

Growing up, I was surrounded by intelligent and encouraging women and men who not only taught me the value of integrity and perseverance, but the power of the female voice and female leadership. Family values are at the core of my political ideals. I truly believe that my strength and tenacity have their foundation in the amazing women I surround myself with, and the extraordinary male support that has given me a truly great perspective on gender relations. The voices of those who came before me have guided, but not dictated, how I view American politics and America's need for female leadership.

The essence of America is opportunity, but, as a nation, we are quickly abusing the opportunity to be the country responsible for the globalization of peace and justice. Our past leaders have shaped a history of vicious power and have exploited our democracy for corrupt, personal aims. Women have been an untapped resource in government and leadership roles. I believe in the power and honesty of female leadership, and I believe that women—especially I—would bring the ideal leadership to our nation, one that does not love power merely for its own sake, but for the ability to expand our country's opportunities.

They say you should never regret or criticize the past, but turn the grave mistakes into life lessons. In the past, our country has recognized

DID YOU KNOW?

✪ Feminism is often described by its historical periods or "waves." First Wave feminists fought for and gained women's right to vote.

✪ Beginning in the 1960s, Second Wave feminists fought for equal opportunity in the work force and a legal ban against gender discrimination.

✪ Since the early 1990s, Third Wave feminists, who believe that issues important to women change from generation to generation and from woman to woman, have encouraged women to be activists, promoting agendas they have defined individually for themselves as "feminist."

the value of education and educational institutions, but has done little to make meaningful improvements. If we plan on putting the future of our country into the hands of younger generations, we must begin to place the highest value on reforming our educational institutions at basic levels. If we fundamentally change our schools, we can begin to change the way children are socialized and learn the politics of race, class, gender, and power. If we provide more funding and quality educators and supplies to public schools, learning will become natural and a means of eradicating violence and discrimination. The Bush administration has put too much emphasis on foreign affairs and global power, and not enough on domestic needs and reform at fundamental levels. We must begin to recognize that change starts at the micro-levels, beginning with the young minds in America.

With the power and honesty of female leadership, America would see many great changes. I hope and truly believe that there will be women before me to serve in the White House, but if there are none, I hope to be the first and pave the way for many generations of female leaders.

REPRESENTATIVE
CANDICE MILLER

(MI)

I'VE LEARNED THAT to represent people you have to listen first. You have to run on issues you are passionate about and feel you can enact a positive change. Promote your strengths and work on your weaknesses. Women are more likely to be successful by taking the time to really understand the people they want to represent and thereby being able to provide honest, positive leadership.

Do researches political history at the San Francisco Public Library.

LYNNA LAN TIEN NGUYEN DO

Age 31

Fremont, California

Year eligible to run: 2012

I will focus on domestic issues first. If our house is a mess, how can we tell others how to clean their homes?

Just ask anybody I meet: One of the first things I tell them is that I want to be president of the United States. This has been true since I was five years old and I first told my parents that I wanted to be president, after I became a doctor. I am still on that path: I am working on my Ph.D. in Political Psychology right now; I already have a B.A. in Politics and a Master's in Public Administration; and I have attended the Women's Campaign School at Yale.

Since my "declaration" at age five, I have aspired to be president for many different reasons. The main reason is to ensure equality for every citizen of the United States. I also want to build better relationships with other countries of the world. Furthermore, I believe it is time that the United States had a woman president, and why not me? I think it is hypocritical of the United States to tout our equality and democracy when, in our short history, we have not had a woman in the top political office—yet other countries that are not democratic, and which do not treat their women as equal to men, have had women in positions of power.

Politics has affected my life on many different planes—the first and most influential effect on my life was being born in the United States. My parents are refugees from Vietnam; my mother was pregnant with me when she and my father left that country right after the fall of Saigon. Had the United States not been involved in Vietnam and fighting there, I might have been born somewhere else.

DID YOU KNOW?

⊛ The Fall of Saigon occurred on April 30, 1975, when North Vietnamese forces captured Saigon, the capital of South Vietnam. The evacuation of American military and civilian personnel was accompanied by a mass exodus of Vietnamese refugees.

⊛ Including tuition and room and board, a four-year education at a public university costs 28 percent of the median family income.

⊛ A four-year education at a private university costs 76 percent of the median family income.

⊛ In the past 25 years, the average cost of college increased 439 percent, while median family income rose only 147 percent.

⊛ Since 2000, the cost of attending public four-year colleges and universities has increased from 39 percent to 55 percent of the income of families in the lowest-income group (the bottom 20 percent of the population).

Source: "Measuring Up 2008," National Center for Public Policy and Higher Education.

Immediately after graduating from college, I started working in politics. My first job was as an assistant in Senator Dianne Feinstein's office in San Francisco. From there, I went on to work for a couple of county supervisors and a mayor, and I recently worked on Gavin Newsom's campaign for mayor of San Francisco. Besides working full time for elected officials, I have become greatly active in the California State Democratic Party, as well as in local and federal political groups and organizations. I also ran an unsuccessful campaign for my local school board.

If I am elected president, I will focus on domestic issues first. If our house is a mess, how can we tell others how to clean their homes? Foreign affairs are important—don't get me wrong—but we need to put some emphasis on our country first and use the state of our domestic affairs to measure how involved we should be in other countries' affairs.

As president, I would also provide a means for our future generations to attend college without amassing a huge amount of debt before they even enter the workforce. I would set a two-year civil service requirement for all high school graduates, and those who choose to go to college and graduate can do another two years of civil service. During these two to four years, the graduates will participate in some form of public service to our country, be it military service, teaching, park service, etc. As they do their duty, they will earn a stipend that will go toward their higher education choice, whether it is a four-year college, technical school, or professional school. I believe it is important to instill a sense of civic duty and social responsibility in each and every citizen of this country.

I have dedicated a lot of time to thinking about what I would do if I were president of the United States. I have thought of all the people I would like to surround me in my cabinet and be my advisors. I know being president is sometimes a thankless job and is highly stressful—but as the saying goes, somebody has to do it—and I would be honored if someday the people of this country would have the faith in me to be their leader and help guide our country to fulfill its great potential.

REPRESENTATIVE
VIRGINIA FOXX

(NC)

YES, IT IS true that if you haven't already encountered bias against you as a woman, you probably will soon. Never let that discourage you or stop you from reaching your goals; instead it can make you stronger, and your success will be all the more meaningful and satisfying. As you pursue your dreams, be sure you make a priority to gain a broad, yet deep education; tap into the network of successful women and men who are everywhere around you; and before you make the leap to public service, develop strategic work experiences that will prepare you to be an effective public servant.

CAMERON RUSSELL

Age 19

Cambridge, Massachusetts

Year eligible to run: 2024

President Clinton told me to work hard, learn as much as I could, and meet many different kinds of people.

DRAWN TO THE LARGE-SCALE DIVERSITY OF NEW YORK CITY, RUSSELL RECENTLY TRANSFERRED FROM WELLESLEY COLLEGE TO COLUMBIA UNIVERSITY.

I've always looked for solutions to the world's problems. When I was three, it was taking the homeless home. By five, it was thinking up an economic policy for Africa (couldn't they sell fossils to tourists?). At eight, I mailed my allowance to the White House to help pay for health care. By twelve, my voter base was well established enough that, through only two degrees of separation, I found myself face to face with Bill Clinton. "I want to become president. Do you have any advice?" I asked him. He told me to work hard, learn as much as I could, and meet many different kinds of people. And so I do:

I met Isabel, who said she was lucky to live in Paramos, Guatemala. She knew many girls who had to walk muddy mountain paths for an hour to get to a washing place. Her *mami* told her that to study hard and to learn English were the most important things. Every day when the sun came up she worked in the cornfields and carried her brother until the sun went down. Then she read her books and fed her brother. When she was fourteen, she won an English essay-writing contest. She was given a computer and tuition for high school. The night before the first school day, the sun went down, and she fed her brother and her *mami* ironed her newly washed clothes. Her *mami* said, "This is what I've always wanted for you." But when Isabel got to school the professor yelled at her, saying that she had to wear a uniform, not dirty indigenous clothing. She bought one with all her money and hid it from her mother. One day she came home to find her brother crying and unattended and her *mami* soaking her feet. Her *mami* said she couldn't go back to school, and she didn't want to.

I met Jeremy, who grew up in Indiana with his father, mother, and eight brothers. His first memory is of his oldest brother coming home in an Army uniform looking like the cleanest thing there was. In time, his other seven brothers all came home standing up straight and shining. "They were enlisted," he was told. His father told him that when he grew up he could either work on the farm or join the Army, too. In first grade, he had to draw a picture of his family. He drew his mother helping his father in the field and himself and his eight brothers in their uniforms, waving as if they'd just come home. His father was so pleased he paid to have the picture framed, and it still hangs above their kitchen table, where Jeremy filled out his application to the Naval Academy. His father is proud because Jeremy could be the first to go to college. And if he doesn't get in, he can always work on the farm or enlist.

And I met Sasha. In kindergarten Sasha learned the hula dance as part of the required Hawaiian curriculum. At eleven, her goldfish died, and she cried for two days. When she was twelve, her dad, a muralist, died of a drug overdose, and Sasha tattooed goldfish on her back to remind her to keep things in perspective. When she turned fifteen, her mom told her she was old enough to support herself, so she took jobs at the local Dairy Queen, Erotic Sex Shop, and a car garage. At eighteen, she came home to a suddenly empty apartment—her so-called friends had sold all her belongings for heroin. Sasha thought it was a joke when she was scouted as a model at age twenty-one and was told Calvin Klein wanted her for their advertising campaign. Maybe she'll go back to college.

These are my peers who won't become president. They are some of the people I have met who have made me understand that becoming president isn't trivial or in the grasp of many people, but it might be for me. My childhood dream has become my adult dream. I have the opportunity, the ability, and the passion to be a leader of my generation.

DID YOU KNOW?

★ After almost three centuries as a Spanish colony, Guatemala won its independence in 1821. During the second half of the twentieth century, it experienced a variety of military and civilian governments, as well as a 36-year guerrilla war. In 1996, the government signed a peace agreement formally ending the conflict, which had left more than 100,000 people dead and had created, by some estimates, some one-million refugees.

★ Hawaii is the fiftieth state, admitted to the Union on August 21, 1959. Hawaii's governor since 2002 has been Republican Linda Lingle. She is the first woman and first person of Jewish ancestry to be governor of the Aloha State.

★ Residents of Indiana are known as Hoosiers, for reasons unknown. Famous Hoosiers include Presidents Benjamin Harrison, William Henry Harrison, and Abraham Lincoln; composers Hoagy Carmichael and Cole Porter; novelists Theodore Dreiser and Kurt Vonnegut; athletic coaches Knute Rockne, Larry Bird, and Don Mattingly; journalists Jane Pauley and Ernie Pyle; food purveyors Orville Redenbacher and Colonel Harland Sanders; actors Steve McQueen and James Dean; actresses Carole Lombard and Florence Henderson; singers Michael Jackson and Axl Rose; vehicle designers Clement Studebaker and Wilbur Wright; and comedians Red Skelton and David Letterman.

REPRESENTATIVE
MARY FALLIN

🐘 (OK)

As Oklahoma's first woman lieutenant governor and only the second woman elected to Congress from the state since 1920, I know how hard it is to break through the glass ceiling while balancing work and family. The best piece of advice I can offer women aspiring to public service is this: People don't care how much you know until they know how much you care. If you are passionate about helping the people around you, then the sky is the limit.

"With a record number of women in Congress and other leadership positions, recent history suggests there are no bounds to what we can accomplish. For all the women out there reading this book: Now is your time to shine!

ERIN MALLORY KIRTON

Age 13

Boulder, Colorado

Year eligible to run: 2032

As president, I would make sure people know that every life is worth saving.

KIRTON PRACTICES FOR A LACROSSE GAME.

"The president is not only the leader of a party, he is the president of the whole people. He must interpret the conscience of America. He must guide his conduct by the idealism of our people," said President Herbert Hoover. If I were president of the United States, I would be careful to do this: listen to what the citizens have to say, and find where our country needs help.

I want to be president because there are many parts of our world today that need change. If we do not change our policies to keep pace with this changing world, we could destroy the world. Therefore, as president, I would promote sustainable energy. I would always help people facing genocide. The West always says, "Never again." Yet, right now, the West is ignoring the genocide in Darfur, Sudan. I would never break my promises to other countries, and that would mean making only very well-thought-out promises. I want to make the United States stick to our original ideals.

Politics has greatly affected my life and my future. Title IX is one of the first ways it has changed my life. I play at least two sports each season, sometimes three. Without Title IX, I couldn't do this. Politics has also given me the right to vote when I am 18. Politics shapes my reputation abroad—currently Americans don't have a very good reputation in many parts of the world. Politics has given me freedom of speech. This is my most valued right.

As president, my main action would be to change the way our government attacks problems. There are four different aspects to every problem:

economic, political, social, and environmental. They all tie together, and when one aspect fails, so do all the others. Currently, the government is looking at mainly the political aspect of our problems. For example, with the war in Iraq, the Bush administration replaced a dictatorship with a democratic republic. For this new government to succeed, it needs moderate Muslims on its side, or the radicals will destroy it. The way to get moderates on our side is to give them well-paying jobs and to prove to them that a democratic republic will help them. It will be easier to do this if we utilize their resources for their benefit, which brings in the environmental aspect. Socially, we need to learn more about the way Iraqis live, so that we understand their rules and traditions. We need to respect their laws and understand that it is these laws and traditions that keep everyone from being the same. By considering the four aspects—economic, political, social, and environmental—we can solve any problem.

Too often countries that have helped us win conflicts are left in ruins. Then they ask us to help pull them out of the ruins, and we turn them down. As a result, their children are taught to hate the United States, and cruel leaders are born. A perfect example of this is Afghanistan after the Cold War. Osama bin Laden worked for us then, and we funded him. After we left the area in ruins, he turned against us and rose in power. We cannot break our promises and leave countries in ruins anymore.

As president, I would make sure people know that every life is worth saving. Being president is a big job, but I believe that with a positive attitude and hope, I would make a good president.

DID YOU KNOW?

⭐ Title IX is part of education legislation enacted in 1972. By ending legal gender discrimination in federally funded public schools, Title IX improved girls' access to academic programs such as science and math education, health care and extracurricular programs, and athletics.

⭐ Since the passage of Title IX, female high school athletic participation has increased by 904 percent.

MURRY MARCHES IN PROTEST OF AN ANTIGAY ORGANIZATION AT ITS ANNUAL CONVENTION IN IRVING, TEXAS.

JOURNEY MURRY

Age 18

Abilene, Texas

Year eligible to run: 2024

" I am deeply devoted to my country. But I also realize that no country is perfect, and improvement is always necessary. Dissent is patriotic. "

*L*ike most kids' career aspirations, mine changed every week when I was young. I wanted to be a queen (not a princess!), or a firefighter, or a veterinarian. Once I reached middle school, I had pretty much settled on wanting to be a teacher. I loved the school environment and couldn't imagine leaving it. Exactly *what* subject I wanted to teach then became the changing factor. For the longest time, I wanted to teach English. Then I fell in love with journalism and creative writing, and I was sure that's what I should teach. I briefly thought about becoming involved in politics, but I wasn't sure if I'd enjoy it, and the idea of directly affecting teen's lives as a teacher appealed to me.

My goals radically shifted when I stepped into the spotlight at my school in Abilene, Texas, where I tried to establish a gay-straight alliance— a club for students of all sexual orientations who want to build bridges between gay and straight teens and discuss issues concerning them. Most students didn't seem to care one way or the other, but my school administration was very opposed to it, giving ridiculous reasons, like "it would promote sexual activity." During the year and a half I fought for the gay-straight alliance, I attended and spoke at numerous school board meetings and gave interviews for the local newspaper and TV stations. When the school board decided to ban all noncurricular clubs rather than allow a gay-straight alliance, I found a lawyer and was prepared to take legal action. Unfortunately, my dad's job transferred him to Lubbock, Texas, and I had to drop my fight.

But now, I had changed. I had gone from being shy and reserved to enjoying discussions and debates about ideas, beliefs, laws, and what is and what should be. I enjoyed presenting myself in front of the school board; I enjoyed answering questions from the media. I was now informed on legal issues, students' rights, precedents for current civil/equal rights movements—and I excelled in my U.S. Government as well as Economics classes, with averages just below 100 in both.

DID YOU KNOW?

★ Among the thirty developed member countries of the OECD, the United States has the largest income inequality—that is, gap between rich and poor citizens—and highest poverty rate, after Mexico and Turkey. The gap in the U.S. has increased rapidly since 2000.

Source: OECD Report, "Growing Unequal?" October 2008.

★ Out of 500 gay teens in 32 states, 69 percent reported some form of harassment or violence against them, according to a 1999 report by the Gay Lesbian Straight Education Network (www.glsen.org).

★ The experiences of many gay teens who endured discrimination and violence against them in high school were documented in a 2001 report by Human Rights Watch, "Hatred in the Hallways: Discrimination and Violence Against Lesbian, Gay, Bisexual, and Transgender Students in U.S. Public Schools" (www.hrw.org/reports/2001/uslgbt).

Law and social issues are my true passions now. I am currently attending Birmingham-Southern College in Alabama as a Political Science major. I hope to go on to law school after that, and I currently intern in a legal department. My very long-term goal is to run for public office—representative or senator—and eventually run for president of the United States. In November 2006, I volunteered with independent Kinky Friedman's campaign for governor of Texas. He didn't win, but I loved the experience and would love to volunteer for a political campaign again.

I know my bid for president will not be an easy one. Besides being a woman, I am also a lesbian and a very outspoken liberal. But I feel that I'm what this country needs. I am deeply devoted to my country. I love our ideals, the different cultures in different states, and the diversity of the people. But I also realize that no country is perfect, and improvement is always necessary. Dissent *is* patriotic.

I believe our country needs to pay more attention to and care more for the disabled and the poor—the gap between rich and poor is still growing. We need better education all around for our students—from actually teaching, instead of just teaching for tests, to better sex education, because lying or withholding information doesn't do anyone any good. War is a drain on our economy, our soldiers, and the families left behind, and should be used only as a last resort. And we need equal rights and equal treatment for all, no matter the age, sex, gender identity, sexual orientation, race, disability, or political affiliation.

These are the ideals the United States is supposed to embrace, and it's about time we have a president who upholds them.

CATHERINE "KAYTE" HOPE KENNEDY

Age 27

Washington, D.C.

Year eligible to run: 2016

> *I would position issues of social justice and equality at the center of all discussions, from taxes to education to international trade.*

KENNEDY EXPLAINS TO THE GIRL SCOUTS OF CHANTILLY, VIRGINIA, HOW TO USE A COMPASS.

I didn't grow up in a very political family, so when I could vote for president for the first time in 2000, I felt debilitatingly overwhelmed. What were the issues? Where did the candidates stand? Where did I stand? A mentor advised me to write a short list of the issues that were important to me and base my decision on them. Taking her advice, I put at the top of my list women's rights, support for the country's less fortunate, positive international relations, and environmental issues. That election took place the same semester I added women's studies to my degree, which provided me with a new way to view the injustices of the world. I eventually moved to Washington, D.C., and became involved with political activism on a national level. I worked with the Feminist Majority Foundation and the Girl Scouts of the USA to empower women and girls. Political activism has become my vocation in both a strong political way—through protesting, letter writing, and campaign organizing—and in more subtle ways—through empowering young girls in Girl Scouting, conversations with friends, and educating myself continually about the issues.

In an attempt to better understand the world outside the United States, I taught English in Santiago, Chile, for almost a year. I chose Chile because I not only wanted to learn Spanish, but I also wanted to be close to the newly elected female president, Michelle Bachelet. I knew it would be interesting to observe the country at this time. If I were president, the first thing I would do is exactly what Michelle Bachelet did—I would appeint a gender-equal cabinet and would ask my nominees to pledge to do the same when hiring their staff.

A more difficult goal to achieve as president would be to remain true to my style of leadership as a woman. My past experiences as president of the activity council in my university have helped me to realize that I work best by empowering the team around me, not through hierarchical command. Bachelet has commented that "usually women who get involved in politics use … men's kind of leadership." The current system in the United States (as well as in Chile) is based on chain of command; leaders who place teamwork at the center are seen as weak and indecisive, a problem that Bachelet has faced. Finding a balance between the two leadership styles would take a lot of work, but it is important to achieving national gender equity and would be central to my personal goals and the goals of my policies.

I want to be president to change the priorities of the White House. I would position issues of social justice and equality at the center of all discussions, from taxes to education to international trade. While talking with Chileans, I noticed there is a genuine concern with how policies affect the country's less fortunate. People are critical of current policies and want to see all citizens succeed. As

DID YOU KNOW?

✪ Zimbabwe has the highest national debt when measured as a percentage of GDP. By this measure, the U.S. ranks twenty-seventh. The U.S. has the highest national debt by dollar amount.

✪ The poorest three countries, each having a per capita annual GDP of less than $1,000, are Malawi, Somalia, and Comoros.

✪ The richest three countries in terms of per capita income are Norway, Switzerland, and the United States.

✪ The most generous countries in terms of per capita donor aid are Luxembourg, Denmark, and Norway. The United States ranks eighteenth.

Source: *CIA World Factbook*, 2007 figures.

president I would work to empower Americans to view government policies in a similarly critical way and to be more actively involved in public affairs between elections. I believe well-rounded, intelligent, and practical discussions would lead to effective policies that would promote good education for everyone, realistic reproductive rights, environmental sustainability, and partner rights for all couples. I also believe these issues can be reasonably implemented while maintaining a healthy economy. My service as president would be to find a way.

As an economic power and a highly educated country, the United States has a responsibility to work toward positive globalization. I believe in the importance of global trade; however, at the same time I'm cautious of how trade policies affect the people of all countries. Canceling the massive debt of countries, especially those in Africa, is an effective way to begin empowering developing economies. As president I would work with representatives of other countries to develop mutually beneficial relationships that also focus on social equality. I would never refuse to meet with a head of state, because personal meetings, both symbolically and practically, resolve problems.

The United States is an influential country that has the potential to positively affect the lives of so many people. As a female president I would build on this potential to promote social equality throughout the world.

KELLY ANNE TULLY

Age 16

New York, New York

Year eligible to run: 2028

> *The policies of men will not be changed if I become president, but the lack of policy for women will.*

TULLY INTERNS FOR SENATOR HILLARY CLINTON, PICTURED HERE GIVING A PRESIDENTIAL CAM-
PAIGN SPEECH AT THE TOWN HALL OF NEW YORK CITY.

I want to be president of the United States. I have always loved politics, government, and law. They are what unify this nation, and support and aid people under a system of well-developed rules and regulations. The only problem I have with this government is its lack of female representation. For over 200 years we have had mostly men in government, and we have had a Civil War and two World Wars. Our presidents have dragged us into such wars as the Vietnam War and the present Iraq war, where diplomacy was merely tolerated until attack plans could be finalized. I truly believe that women have a gigantic role to play in helping this country succeed in reaching its goals and avoiding such wars.

The United States is ranked only sixty-fifth in the world in terms of the number of female representatives in its national government. That is unbelievable. For such a powerful country based on democracy, justice, and equality for all, the fact that women are so underrepresented is deplorable.

I have grown up around politics, as all my family members are active participants, and are fascinated by it. In turn, I have become involved. I have interned for Senator Hillary Clinton, who is a force to be reckoned with. So I understand the realities of a high-powered political job. It is not all glamour and glitz; in many ways politics is a shrewd game that can be based on lies and malicious attacks. It is unfortunate, but it is a reality. Anyone who wants to be a politician has got to be tough and confident in his or her beliefs, but a woman who wants to do the job must be twice as tough and twice as confident, because the reality is that women are forced into a disadvantage by our patriarchal society. Women who accept such a tough role and stay on top and maintain their morals and confidence deserve the office; they deserve every goal they reach for. At the ripe old age of 16, I cannot pretend that I have this tough exterior already; it is not innate. But my passion for politics and for seeing a woman in the highest office in the land gives me an intense resolve at a young age.

If I were president I would prioritize changing this almost impulsive attitude toward violence. Too often have presidents said after wartime is over that they should have used violence as a last resort. TV shows such as "24" display torture as if it were a common and effective tool for the protection of our country; it is not. Diplomacy is the best policy, and maintaining such an attitude and keeping our troops safe are really what "supporting the troops" should mean.

There is a joke that if men could get pregnant, abortions would not only be legal, but federally funded as well. It is no secret that men and women are different, so how is it possible that men understand the lives of women? For far too long women's needs have been marginalized by the men in power. The policies of men will not be changed if I become president, but the lack of policy for women will.

In the end, being president should have little to do with one's gender, but instead with one's competency, ideas, and beliefs. I should be allowed to pursue my political aspirations, grand or small, free from gender discrimination. I believe that this nation may be at a point where gender and race cannot make or break a candidate. Finally.

 DID YOU KNOW?

The following countries have female heads of state (as of December 2008):

- ✪ **ARGENTINA:** Cristina E. Fernández de Kirchner, Executive President, 2007-present
- ✪ **CHILE:** Michelle Bachelet Jeria, Executive President, 2006-present
- ✪ **FINLAND:** Tarja Halonen, President, 2000-present
- ✪ **GERMANY:** Angela Merkel, Federal Chancellor, 2005-present
- ✪ **INDIA:** Pratibha Patil, President, 2007-present
- ✪ **IRELAND:** Mary McAleese, President, 1997-present
- ✪ **LIBERIA:** Ellen Johnson-Sirleaf, Executive President, 2006-present
- ✪ **THE PHILIPPINES:** Gloria Macapagal-Arroyo, Executive President, 2001-present

JENNIFER ABRACZINSKAS

Age 22

Catawissa, Pennsylvania

Year eligible to run: 2024

" My patriotism is not blind,

and this is why I want to

serve in public office. "

DURING A BREAK FROM LA SALLE UNIVERSITY, ABRACZINSKAS STROLLS THROUGH HER FAMILY'S CHRISTMAS TREE FARM.

A sense of service to the nation grows naturally in American small towns. There is no denying the feeling of freedom in open fields or the surge of patriotism I feel as I pass by house after house flying the Stars and Stripes in the morning sunshine. At home, in Catawissa, Pennsylvania, there is sense of camaraderie that causes neighbors to care for one another, trust in the choices of the majority, and prize justice and liberty. The American dream seems very real to me: My house is built on one of the farms that is part of my family's Christmas tree business—an enterprise originated at the turn of the twentieth century by my great-great-grandfather Andrew, an immigrant from Lithuania. When I see the offices of the business each morning, I am reminded that the richness of my life is the result of past generations' hard work and dedication and the opportunities of this country.

My college years in Philadelphia, a summer internship in New York City, and frequent visits to Washington, D.C., have shown me that big city buildings and bustle are a result of individuals trying to make better lives for themselves and their families. With so many people living and working together, organizing and specializing, there is an amazing array of health care services, business opportunities, and educational and cultural offerings that we all can enjoy. American ingenuity and enterprise, compassion, and ideas thrive in U.S. cities.

My patriotism is not blind, however, and this is why I want to serve in public office. Many times I have been disappointed in what I have come across in our nation. I met a woman who, after receiving a high school diploma, was only semiliterate, and after years of working in manufacturing found herself both jobless, due to factory relocation, and unemployable, due to her substandard education. When mentoring students in a Philadelphia middle school, I heard stories of gunshots keeping families up at night and kids being afraid to walk to school in the morning; these students were stuck in the neighborhoods where several of the 400 citywide murders occurred last year. And while volunteering in a nonprofit health clinic, I saw countless patients who delayed seeking help for their health crises because they work two or three jobs and receive no health insurance. Each time I hear one of these stories or look at the children playing in vacant lots next to crumbling buildings, I think: We can do better.

I have had the opportunity to travel to many other countries during my college career. There, too, I found mixed American reviews. Many of the students I talked with admired our justice system and our quality roads, buildings, and education, and even envied our ability to question our government and our president. Yet our foreign policy was always called into question. Students I met in Thailand were incredulous that our country, so interested in freedom, would invade another. In a Chilean shantytown, a ghost from our past was still very real to students trying to rebuild their communities after the fall of dictator Augusto Pinochet. After visiting concentration camps that held political prisoners during his reign, I saw why they were outraged with our support of Pinochet and why they questioned our newest military endeavors a world away. In Tanzania and India, I was more upset than my foreign colleagues by the extreme poverty and illness I saw there despite growing efforts to boost their economies. I believe we can only benefit from the prosperity of our global neighbors, and in that respect, we can do better to ensure that every person has the opportunity to live.

Like people, countries continually make judgment calls attempting to advance the welfare of their people. And, like any one person's decisions, even mine, some of our country's decisions result

DID YOU KNOW?

★ After soaring in 2007, the murder rate in Philadelphia dropped by about 20 percent as of October 2008, by which time more than 250 Philadelphians had been murdered during the year.

★ According to the FBI, an estimated 1,408,337 violent crimes occurred nationwide in 2007.

★ There were an estimated 466.9 violent crimes per 100,000 inhabitants.

★ When data for 2007 were compared with 2006 data, the estimated volume of violent crime declined 0.7 percent.

★ Aggravated assault accounted for 60.8 percent of violent crimes, the highest number of violent crimes reported to law enforcement. Robbery comprised 31.6 percent, and rape accounted for 6.4 percent. Murder accounted for 1.2 percent of estimated violent crimes in 2007.

in beneficial outcomes, while others have terrible effects. The greatest characteristic of the United States is our ability to change and make better those mistakes of the past, and I want to be part of that change.

I cannot begin to guess what policy issues will be most important when I run for office, but I believe that keeping the American people—and people in general—at the forefront of decision making will result in the best outcomes for our country. I would like to prepare Americans to thrive by providing an education that is strong enough to allow individuals to compete in local and global labor markets and to appreciate the diversity of our nation, which will only increase with our advances in communication technology and transportation. I believe that every American should have the right to be healthy and have access to quality health care. With more research and development, we must find and implement a system—whether public or private—that allows for progress in medicine without risking the health of any of our citizens. We must encourage businesses to grow and help reinvent the American economy so that we can prosper with the rise of other economies globally. We need to focus on waste treatment, recycling, and clean energy to preserve the natural beauty of our country and our world. And I would love to implement a foreign policy of which we can all be proud. Our foreign policy should make us an example to the rest of the world; it should entail a sincere commitment to the United Nations, and should provide a hand up for our global neighbors, recognizing that equality and justice should not be confined by national boundaries, but rather, are inalienable rights. The spread of disease and global climate change have shown us that we are all in this boat together; we should sail together.

I am twenty-two years old and am charting the path of my life, which now entails applying to medical school. I know I need to learn much more before I can become a national leader, but I am willing to commit to this country because of what I already know. I believe in the people of this nation—in their resilience, in their desire to work hard, and in their belief in justice and equality. I know our strength lies in our foundation of freedom, in our capacity to change, and in our diversity. And, regardless of gender, ethnicity, or origin, we are all stewards of the promise of our Constitution—to serve and be served by the United States of America. So when I have the opportunity to run for office—for state house, national Senate, or even president—I will not look to others to carry that commitment for me. Rather, I will remember the words of a Hopi elder: "Be good to each other and do not look outside yourself for the leader.... We are the ones we have been waiting for."

HANNAH L. KUHN-GALE

Age 7

Fort Collins, Colorado

Year eligible to run: 2036

> *A person should be free*
>
> *to believe in a god,*
>
> *in a spirit, or in no god.*

KUHN-GALE IS ALWAYS READY TO MARCH FOR A CAUSE SHE BELIEVES IN.

My name is Hannah. I am seven and a half and I am in second grade. I live in Fort Collins, Colorado. I have a younger sister named Haley who is three. I like to play tennis and soccer. I love animals and have a bunny, a beta fish, and a water frog. I would like to run for president in 2036 because then I would be over thirty-five years old. There has never been a woman president. If I am not elected president, hopefully I will at least see a woman president in my lifetime. I feel that it is unfair that men have been prejudiced and have not let there be a woman president. Maybe I will be the first one! I think a woman should be president because women can do just as good a job as men and because women are just as smart as men are.

If I were president, I would not want there to be war, then we would have less killing and everybody could have a peaceful life. I would not like people to carry weapons around. They might kill people, and that is sort of like war. I would also want everything to be fair. For instance, gays and lesbians, women, minorities, and disabled people should all have the same rights as everybody else. I would want people to take care of the Earth and each other. People should help others who are having a hard time. If people are homeless, we should take care of them. For example, we should be able to give them a meal or find them a place to stay for the night. As president, I would also protect animals. If there were no animals, it would be a pretty dull world.

I think everyone should be able to believe whatever he or she chooses without being judged by other people. A person should be free to believe in a god, in a spirit, or in no god.

If I were president, I would say, "Let's raise money so people could have a peaceful and happy life." I would ask those who are really rich to give some of their money to other people. I would try to convince them by telling them how many people there are who need homes, food, and clothes. They should give a little extra to help children. If they did this, I would ask factories to make medals for them that say, "I saved people's lives!"

Finally, I would like to see women meet and protest, so that hopefully someday soon there will be a woman president!

DID YOU KNOW?

Americans describe themselves as having the following religious affiliations:

CHRISTIAN: 79.8 percent

NO RELIGION/ATHEIST/AGNOSTIC:
15.0 percent

JEWISH: 1.4 percent

MUSLIM: 0.6 percent

BUDDHIST: 0.5 percent

HINDU: 0.4 percent

UNITARIAN UNIVERSALIST: 0.3 percent

OTHER RELIGIONS: 0.7 percent

Source: City University of New York, *American Religious Identification Survey 2001.*

CHELSEA ANN ZIMMERMAN

Age 18

Minneapolis, Minnesota

Year eligible to run: 2024

"*It would be a refreshing change to see government leaders who collaborate and compromise rather than dictate, who encourage open debate rather than reward blind loyalty.*"

ZIMMERMAN ONCE SERVED HERE, IN THE MINNESOTA HOUSE OF REPRESENTATIVES, AS A PAGE.

I remember hatching the plan to run for president of the United States one day while paging through *Free to Be ... You and Me* for the hundredth time. I had briefly considered other occupations, including firefighter, professional football player, and even race car driver. But I was tantalized by the possibility of leading others, meeting foreign dignitaries, and, I have to confess, living in a house that has its own bowling alley.

The dream to become president stuck with me; never did my parents even once suggest that this might be an unattainable goal. Over time, close friends and teachers learned of my ambition to occupy the Oval Office and offered encouragement, promising to enlist as volunteers in my campaign.

My presidential aspirations opened doors for me as word spread of my interest in politics; everyone wants to help a fresh face willing to work hard with enthusiasm and passion for her causes. From the time I was in junior high school I have run for student office, door-knocked during political campaigns, and even convinced friends to hold signs for candidates at busy intersections on Election Day. I witnessed politics in action when I served as a page at the Minnesota State Legislature and worked for a woman who is now speaker of the Minnesota House of Representatives.

Last fall, when entering Barnard College, I decided to throw my hat into the ring for class president and won the election. The highlight of my first year in college has been working with a student government

DID YOU KNOW?

✪ *Free to Be... You and Me* is a 1972 recorded album and illustrated songbook for children. It was performed by celebrities in 1974 as the television special "Marlo Thomas and Friends." Using poetry, songs, and sketches, the performers promoted values such as individuality, tolerance, and happiness with one's identity. Its main message is that anyone, whether a boy or a girl, can achieve anything one wants.

✪ The White House Bowling Alley is a one-lane bowling alley in the basement of the White House. Bowling lanes were first built in the ground floor of the West Wing as a birthday gift for President Truman in 1947 (in the location of the present-day Situation Room); Truman didn't care for bowling himself but allowed his staff to start a league. In 1969, President and Mrs. Nixon, both avid bowlers, had a new one-lane alley built (paid for by friends) in an underground workspace area below the driveway leading to the North Portico. As of press time, rumor has it that President Obama is considering replacing the bowling alley with a basketball court.

made up of strong, articulate, supportive women who long ago figured out that women can be powerful leaders.

As president of the United States, I will bring my experience, qualifications, and compassion to the office. I am acutely aware of the issues that face my generation—global warming and deep-seated international conflicts that have worsened in recent years, as well as poverty and access to health care and education—issues that disproportionately affect women. I would use my power as president to address issues that historically have been given too little attention, such as early childhood health and education funding. I would depart from the practice of past administrations of making appointments from a homogeneous pool of white male candidates. I would strive to open up the channels of power to qualified men and women of all ethnic and racial groups. Historically, women have been underrepresented at all levels of government, and I would work hard to reverse this. In a country with slightly more women than men, our elected leaders should be representative of both genders. Research shows that women have different leadership styles than men. It would be a refreshing change to see government leaders who collaborate and compromise rather than dictate, who encourage open debate rather than reward blind loyalty.

By 2024, when I run for president, the refrain of "there are no qualified women to fill this position" will be erased from our memory. My generation will have created an environment where a woman running for president is no longer a novelty but an inevitable reality.

REPRESENTATIVE
ALLYSON SCHWARTZ

 (PA)

*M*Y POLITICAL ADVICE to young women is the same advice that I give to women of all ages—your individual involvement in politics makes a difference! With more than 30 years of public service experience, I know how much it matters to have women at the table, when crucial decisions affecting all of our lives are being made. Whether it is voting, serving on a board, working for a candidate you believe in, writing your first-ever check to support a campaign, or running for office—do not wait for permission. You should carefully weigh your decisions both personally and professionally, but then take that next step—don't wait. Know why you are running, what you believe in, what you hope to accomplish—and if it is right, go for it.

As the only woman member of Congress currently in Pennsylvania's 19-member delegation, I'm proud to have paved the way for other women across the Commonwealth. I'm optimistic that my political experiences and accomplishments will encourage other women to think of running for office or become more politically active. We need more women, young and older, to get involved, to work on campaigns, to run for office, and to use their strengths, talents, and energy to fight for the values they believe in for our communities, states, and for a great America.

TARA ANDREWS

Age 33

Baltimore, Maryland

Year eligible to run: 2012

My lineage and my legacy

conspire to place a demand

on me that I'm sometimes

slow to embrace but that I

dare not ignore.

When I was fourteen years old I made two decisions that would determine the rest of my life: (1) I would be the baddest criminal defense attorney to ever walk the block, and (2) I would be the first African-American woman president of the United States.

Both decisions were predicated on what I saw occurring in my small hometown of Hamilton, Ohio. On a daily basis, I saw how young black kids, especially the boys, were treated differently from young white kids by the police and the criminal justice system. I determined that these boys needed good defense lawyers. I also determined that someone needed to change the system, and in my fourteen-year-old mind the president of the United States was the most powerful person in the world and, therefore, the one who could make that change happen.

Almost twenty years later, I am still driven by those initial impressions and the convictions that they birthed in me. I am an advocate to my core, always seeking ways to right the system, reprove government for its sins, and fight for fairness and justice. I went to law school. But while working to become a criminal trial attorney, I quickly found that my vision for change was too broad to achieve case by case. I want to change *the system*, which means I have to change the laws and the policies that govern and drive the system. So instead of becoming a trial attorney, I chose to become a policy advocate. And true to my nature, I'm drawn to those issues that have few champions and that most impact "the least of them." Currently, I serve as the Deputy Executive Director for Policy and Programs at the Coalition for Juvenile Justice, a national nonprofit focused on improving government's response to children and youth who come into contact with the juvenile or criminal justice system. I am particularly focused on those policies and practices that negatively impact children of color in disproportionate ways.

That is why I am called even more to our nation's highest office. I have learned that the president is the not the all-powerful person that I once believed him to be. However, he—or she—is still the most powerful person in the world, and alone wields a type of authority and influence that can be used for good—or for evil. In my estimation, too many presidents throughout our history have failed to make full and honorable use of the office. As a result, Americans and the rest of the world have experienced far too much poverty, oppression, and premature death—and far too little peace, abundance, and love. To whom much is given, much is required. Our nation and this world are calling for wise, courageous, and sacrificial leadership. That call intimidates me, humbles me, and *inspires* me to run for president.

So I run. So far, I have run two unsuccessful races for Maryland's state legislature. I've made the rookie mistakes someone would expect a young woman of color with no base, no institution, and no well-connected man standing in front of her or behind her to make. But I run. And I run in spite of myself. I'm melancholy by temperament. I derive no joy from the campaign. The continual meetings tire me; the partisan politics and political games anger me; the constant hunt for endorsements bores me; and the money chase dispirits me. But the work ignites me. The plight of the people provokes me. The small victories that I and like-minded advocates achieve revive me. My lineage and my legacy conspire to place a demand on me that I'm sometimes slow to embrace, but that I dare not ignore.

And I encourage others to run. I volunteer with a local young women's political leadership program called Running Start, through which I mentor women younger than I in order to support them, encourage them, and help them learn from my mistakes.

And I watch. I watch CNN and C-SPAN and MSNBC and Fox News. I watch Hillary and Condi and Kay and Elizabeth. I watch Clinton and Obama and Edwards and Biden. I watch Bush and McCain and Giuliani and Romney. And I listen. And I question. And I pray. Oh, do I pray. And I learn. And I move ever closer to realizing the purpose that was born in me in a little Ohio town almost twenty years ago.

To be president of the United States of America.

Appendixes

35 Current Leaders

At the time this book went to press, there were 104 women serving as governors, senators, congresswomen, and cabinet members. Of these women, plus two from the previous administration, I speculated wildly (or not so wildly in the case of Hillary Clinton) about which 35 are the most likely to eventually run for president.

—Amy Sewell

Governor Sarah Palin (R-AK)

Governor M. Jodi Rell (R-CT)

Governor Kathleen Sebelius (D-KS)

Governor Christine Gregoire (D-WA)

Senator Lisa Murkowski (R-AK)

Senator Blanche Lincoln (D-AR)

Senator Mary Landrieu (D-LA)

Senator Susan Collins (R-ME)

Senator Olympia Snowe (R-ME)

Senator Amy Klobuchar (D-MN)

Senator Claire McCaskill (D-MO)

Senator Kay Hagan (D-NC)

Senator Kirsten Gillibrand (D-NY)

Senator Kay Bailey Hutchison (R-TX)

Representative Gabrielle Giffords (D-AZ)

Representative Ellen Tauscher (D-CA)

Representative Grace Napolitano (D-CA)

Representative Linda Sanchez (D-CA)

Representative Loretta Sanchez (D-CA)

Representative Susan Davis (D-CA)

Representative Diana DeGette (D-CO)

Representative Debbie Wasserman Schultz (D-FL)

Representative Judy Biggert (R-IL)

Representative Candice Miller (R-MI)

Representative Virginia Foxx (R-NC)

Representative Sue Myrick (R-NC)

Representative Mary Fallin (R-OK)

Representative Allyson Schwartz (D-PA)

Representative Stephanie Herseth Sandlin (D-SD)

Representative Marsha Blackburn (R-TN)

Representative Cathy McMorris Rodgers (R-WA)

Secretary of State Hillary Rodham Clinton

Secretary of Homeland Security Janet Napolitano

Former Secretary of State Condoleezza Rice

Former Secretary of Education Margaret Spellings

FEMALE PRESIDENTIAL CANDIDATES: PARTY NOMINEES

YEAR	NAME	PARTY
1872	Victoria Woodhull	Equal Rights Party
1884	Belva Ann Lockwood	National Equal Rights Party
1888	Belva Ann Lockwood	National Equal Rights Party
1940	Gracie Allen	Surprise Party
1952	Ellen Linea W. Jensen	Washington Peace Party
	Mary Kennery	American Party
	Agnes Waters	American Woman's Party
1968	Charlene Mitchell	Communist Party
1972	Linda Jenness	Socialist Workers Party
	Evelyn Reed	Socialist Workers Party
1976	Margaret Wright	People's Party
1980	Ellen McCormack	Right to Life Party
	Maureen Smith	Peace and Freedom Party
	Deirdre Griswold	Workers World Party

YEAR	NAME	PARTY
1984	Sonia Johnson	Citizens Party
	Gavrielle Holmes	Workers World Party
1988	Lenora Fulani	New Alliance Party
	Willa Kenoyer	Socialist Party, Liberty Union Party
1992	Lenora Fulani	New Alliance Party
	Helen Halyard	Socialist Equality Party
	Isabell Masters	Looking Back Party
	Gloria La Riva	Workers World Party
1996	Monica Moorehead	Workers World Party
	Marsha Feinland	Peace and Freedom Party
	Mary Cal Hollis	Socialist Party, Liberty Union Party
	Diane Beall Templin	The American Party
	Isabell Masters	Looking Back Party
2000	Monica Moorehead	Workers World Party
	Cathy Gordon Brown	Independent
2004	Diane Beall Templin	The American Party
2008	Diane Beall Templin	The American Party
	Gloria La Riva	Party for Socialism and Liberation
	Elvena Lloyd-Duffie	Independent
	Cynthia McKinney	Green Party, Workers World Party

Female Vice-Presidential Candidates: Party Nominees

YEAR	NAME	PARTY
1884	Marietta Stow	National Equal Rights Party
1924	Marie Brehm	Prohibition Party
1932	Florence Garvin	National Party
1936	Florence Garvin	Greenback Party
1948	Grace Carlson	Socialist Workers Party
1952	Charlotta Bass	Progressive Party, Communist Party, American Labor Party
	Myra Tanner Weiss	Socialist Workers Party
1956	Georgia Cozzini	Socialist Labor Party
	Myra Tanner Weiss	Socialist Workers Party
	Ann Marie Yezo	American Third Party
1960	Georgia Cozzini	Socialist Labor Party
	Myra Tanner Weiss	Socialist Workers Party

YEAR	NAME	PARTY
1968	Peggy Terry	Peace and Freedom Party
1972	Genevieve Gundersen	Socialist Labor Party
	Theodora B. Nathan	Libertarian Party
1976	Constance Blomen	Socialist Labor Party
	Willie Mae Reid	Socialist Workers Party
1980	Elizabeth Cervantes Barron	Peace and Freedom Party
	Naomi Cohen	Workers World Party
	Angela Davis	Communist Party
	Diane Drufenbrock	Socialist Party
	Wretha Hanson	Citizens Party
	La Donna Harris	Citizens Party
	Gavrielle Holmes	Workers World Party
	Eileen Shearer	American Independent Party
	Matilde Zimmermann	Socialist Workers Party
1984	Jean T. Brust	Socialist Equality Party
	Angela Davis	Communist Party
	Geraldine Ferraro	Democratic Party
	Andrea Gonzales	Socialist Workers Party
	Helen Halyard	Socialist Equality Party
	Gloria La Riva	Workers World Party
	Emma Wong Mar	Peace and Freedom Party
	Nancy Ross	New Alliance Party
	Maureen Kennedy Salaman	Populist Party
	Matilde Zimmermann	Socialist Workers Party
1988	Joan Andrews	Right to Life Party
	Joyce Dattner	New Alliance Party
	Debra Freeman	National Economic Recovery Party

YEAR	NAME	PARTY
1988	Susan Gardner	Consumer Party
	Helen Halyard	Socialist Equality Party
	Gloria La Riva	Workers World Party
	Kathleen Mickells	Socialist Workers Party
	Vikki Murdock	Peace and Freedom Party
1992	Estelle DeBates	Socialist Workers Party
	Doris Feimer	The American Party
	Barbara Garson	Socialist Party
	Nancy Lord	Libertarian Party
	Maria Elizabeth Munoz	New Alliance Party
	Willie Mae Reid	Socialist Workers Party
	Joann Roland	Third Party
	Asiba Tupahache	Peace and Freedom Party
1996	Connie Chandler	Independent Party of Utah
	Laura Garza	Socialist Workers Party
	Anne Goeke	Green Party
	Rosemary Giumarra	Independent
	Madelyn Hoffman	Green Party
	Jo Jorgensen	Libertarian Party
	Rachel Bubar Kelly	Prohibition Party
	Winona LaDuke	Green Party
	Shirley Jean Masters	Looking Back Party
	Anne Northrop	AIDS Cure Party
	Krista Paradise	Green Party
	Kate McClatchy	Peace and Freedom Party
	Muriel Tillinghast	Green Party
2000	Sabrina R. Allen	Independent
	Ezola B. Foster	Reform Party
	Mary Cal Hollis	Socialist Party

YEAR	NAME	PARTY
2000	Winona LaDuke	Green Party
	Gloria La Riva	Workers World Party
	Margaret Trowe	Socialist Workers Party
2004	Marilyn Chambers	Personal Choice Party
	Irene M. Deasy	Independent
	Teresa Gutierrez	Workers World Party, Liberty Union Party
	Arrin Hawkins	Socialist Workers Party
	Mary Alice Herbert	Socialist Party, Natural Law Party
	Janice Jordan	Peace and Freedom Party
	Pat LaMarche	Green Party
	Jennifer A. Ryan	Christian Freedom Party
	Karen Sanchirico	Independent
	Margaret Trowe	Socialist Workers Party
2008	Rosa Clemente	Green Party, Workers World Party
	Alyson Kennedy	Socialist Workers Party
	Sarah Palin	Republican Party
	Andrea Marie Psoras	Vote Here Party
	Patricia Rubacky	New American Independent Party

FEMALE PRESIDENTIAL CANDIDATES WHO FAILED TO RECEIVE THEIR PARTIES' NOMINATION

YEAR	NAME	PARTY	NOMINATION WINNER
1964	Margaret Chase Smith	Republican Party	Barry Goldwater
	Fay T. Carpenter Swain	Democratic Party	Lyndon B. Johnson
1972	Shirley Chisholm	Democratic Party	George McGovern
	Patsy Takamoto Mink	Democratic Party	George McGovern
	Bella Savitzky Abzug	Democratic Party	George McGovern
1976	Barbara Jordan	Democratic Party	Jimmy Carter
	Ellen McCormack	Democratic Party	Jimmy Carter
1980	Koryne Kaneski Horbal	Democratic Party	Jimmy Carter
	Alice Tripp	Democratic Party	Jimmy Carter
1984	Martha Kirkland	Democratic Party	Walter Mondale
1988	Patricia Schroeder	Democratic Party	Michael Dukakis
1992	Georgiana Doerschuck	Republican Party	George H.W. Bush
	Caroline Killeen	Democratic Party	Bill Clinton
	Tennie Rogers	Republican Party	George H.W. Bush

YEAR	NAME	PARTY	NOMINATION WINNER
1996	Georgiana Doerschuck	Republican Party	Bob Dole
	Susan Gail Ducey	Republican Party	Bob Dole
	Elvena E. Lloyd-Duffie	Democratic Party	Bill Clinton
	Dr. Heather Anne Harder	Democratic Party	Bill Clinton
	Caroline Killeen	Democratic Party	Bill Clinton
	Mary "France" LeTulle	Republican Party	Bob Dole
	Isabell Masters	Republican Party	Bob Dole
	Tennie Rogers	Republican Party	Bob Dole
2000	Elizabeth Dole	Republican Party	George W. Bush
	Dr. Heather Anne Harder	Democratic Party	Al Gore
	Angel Joy Chavis Rocker	Republican Party	George W. Bush
	Dorian Yeager	Republican Party	George W. Bush
2004	Katherine Bateman	Democratic Party	John Kerry
	JoAnne Bier Beeman	Green Party	David Cobb
	Sheila Bilyeu	Green Party	David Cobb
	Carol Moseley Braun	Democratic Party	John Kerry
	Jeanne Chebib	Democratic Party	John Kerry
	Mildred T. Glover	Democratic Party	John Kerry
	Caroline Killeen	Democratic Party	John Kerry
	Millie Howard	Republican Party	George W. Bush
	Carol A. Miller	Green Party	David Cobb
	Lorna Salzman	Green Party	David Cobb
	Florence Walker	Democratic Party	John Kerry
2008	Hillary Rodham Clinton	Democratic Party	Barack Obama
	Susan Gail Ducey	Republican Party	John McCain
	Caroline Killeen	Democratic Party	Barack Obama
	Elaine Brown	Green Party	Cynthia McKinney

YEAR	NAME	PARTY	NOMINATION WINNER
2008	Nan Garrett	Green Party	Cynthia McKinney
	Kat Swift	Green Party	Cynthia McKinney
	Mary Ruwart	Libertarian Party	Bob Barr
	Christine Smith	Libertarian Party	Bob Barr

FEMALE VICE-PRESIDENTIAL CANDIDATES WHO FAILED TO RECEIVE THEIR PARTIES' NOMINATION

YEAR	NAME	PARTY	NOMINATION WINNER
1848	Lucretia Mott	Liberty Party	C.C. Foote
1924	Lena Springs	Democratic Party	Charles W. Bryan
1928	Nellie Tayloe Ross	Democratic Party	Joseph T. Robinson
1952	India Edwards	Democratic Party	John Sparkman
	Sarah T. Hughes	Democratic Party	John Sparkman
1972	Shirley Chisholm	Democratic Party	Thomas Eagleton
	Frances Farenthold	Democratic Party	Thomas Eagleton
	Martha Griffiths	Democratic Party	Thomas Eagleton
	Patricia Harris	Democratic Party	Thomas Eagleton
	Eleanor McGovern	Democratic Party	Thomas Eagleton
	Martha Mitchell	Democratic Party	Thomas Eagleton
	Maggie Kuhn	People's Party	Benjamin Spock
1976	Anne Armstrong	Republican Party	Bob Dole
	Barbara Jordan	Democratic Party	Walter Mondale
	Nancy Palm	Republican Party	Bob Dole

YEAR	NAME	PARTY	NOMINATION WINNER
1984	Shirley Chisholm	Democratic Party	Geraldine Ferraro
	Jeane J. Kirkpatrick	Republican Party	George H. W. Bush
1992	Susan K.Y. Shargal	Democratic Party	Al Gore
2008	Mary Alice Herbert	Socialist Party	Stewart Alexander

LEADERSHIP GROUPS AND NONPROFIT ORGANIZATIONS

CENTER FOR AMERICAN WOMEN AND POLITICS

Eagleton Institute of Politics
Rutgers, The State University of New Jersey
191 Ryders Lane
New Brunswick, NJ 08901-8557
(732) 932-9384
Fax: (732) 932-0014
www.rci.rutgers.edu/~cawp/xxindex.html

CENTER FOR THE ADVANCEMENT OF WOMEN

25 West 43rd Street, Suite 1120
New York, NY 10036
(212) 391-7718
Fax: (212) 391-7720
www.advancewomen.org

Led by Faye Wattleton, the Center for the Advancement of Women is a not-for-profit institution dedicated to research-based education and advocacy for women. The Center is an independent, nonpartisan organization founded in 1995, whose mission is to conduct national opinion research among women to measure experiences in their daily lives. This research presents a profile of women that is used to educate opinion leaders, policy makers, and the general public.

COLLEGE REPUBLICAN NATIONAL COMMITTEE

600 Pennsylvania Avenue, SE, Suite 215
Washington, DC 20003

(888) 765-3564
Fax: (202) 608-1429
E-mail: info@crnc.org
www.crnc.org

The College Republican National Committee (CRNC), an independent Section 527 political organization, is the nation's oldest and largest youth political organization. Founded in 1892, the CRNC currently has over a quarter of a million members on over 1,800 campuses nationwide.

The work of the College Republican National Committee is guided by two primary goals: to help elect Republicans and to prepare future leaders of the party. The CRNC serves as the grassroots arm of the Republican Party. The cornerstone of the CRNC's work is its annual Field Program. Full-time, college-age Field Representatives are in charge of recruiting, registering, training, and mobilizing Republicans on college campuses to vote and volunteer in the upcoming election. Their goal is to implement grassroots programs by sending these young political leaders to key districts to help build the party and assist in electing Republicans at nearly every level of government.

EMILY's LIST

1120 Connecticut Avenue NW, Suite 1100
Washington, DC 20036
(202) 326-1400
Fax: (202) 326-1415
E-mail: information@emilyslist.org
www.emilyslist.org

EMILY'S List, the nation's largest grassroots political network, is dedicated to building a progressive America by electing pro-choice Democratic women to federal, state, and local office. It is a network of more than 100,000 Americans—from all across the country—committed to recruiting and funding viable women candidates; helping them build and run effective campaign organizations; training the next generation of activists; and mobilizing women voters to help elect progressive candidates across the nation.

THE FEMINIST MAJORITY FOUNDATION
1600 Wilson Boulevard, Suite 801
Arlington, VA 22209
(703) 522-2214
Fax: (703) 522-2219
www.feminist.org

The Feminist Majority Foundation (FMF) is dedicated to women's equality, reproductive health, and nonviolence. In all spheres, FMF utilizes research and action to empower women economically, socially, and politically. Its research and action programs focus on advancing the legal, social, and political equality of women with men, countering the backlash to women's advancement, and recruiting and training young feminists to encourage future leadership for the feminist movement in the United States.

To carry out these aims, FMF engages in research and public policy development, public education programs, grassroots organizing projects, leadership training, and development programs, and participates in and organizes forums on issues of women's equality and empowerment. Its sister organization, the Feminist Majority, engages in lobbying and other direct political action, pursuing equality between women and men through legislative avenues.

GENERATIONENGAGE
Washington, DC, Headquarters
Presidential Plaza; 900 19th Street, NW
Washington, DC 20006
(202) 986-1223
E-mail: washington@generationengage.org
www.generationengage.org

GenerationEngage is a nonpartisan youth-civic-engagement initiative that connects young Americans to political leaders, to other civic organizations, and to meaningful debate about the future they will inherit. GenerationEngage is built on three principles:

- Young people suffer not from a lack of interest, but from a lack of access
- Our democracy should be a dialogue, not a monologue
- The best investment we can make in the future of democracy is in young leaders at the local level

GIRL SCOUTS OF THE USA
420 Fifth Avenue
New York, NY 10018-2798
(800) GSUSA 4 U [(800) 478-7248] or (212) 852-8000
www.girlscouts.org

Girl Scouts of the USA is the world's preeminent organization dedicated solely to girls—all girls—where, in an accepting and nurturing environment, girls build character and skills for success in the real world. In partnership with committed adult volunteers, girls develop qualities that will serve them all their lives, like leadership, strong values, social conscience, and conviction about their own potential and self-worth.

Founded in 1912 by Juliette Gordon Low, Girl Scouts' membership has grown from 18 members in Savannah, Georgia, to 3.7 million members throughout the United States, including U.S. territories, and in more than 90 countries through USA Girl Scouts Overseas.

GIRLS CLUB OF AMERICA
National Headquarters
1275 Peachtree Street, NE
Atlanta, GA 30309-3506
(404) 487-5700
E-mail: info@bgca.org
www.bgca.org

The mission of the Girls Club of America is to enable all young girls, especially those who need us most, to reach their full potential as productive, caring, responsible citizens.

GIRLS FOR A CHANGE

P.O. Box 1436
San Jose, CA 95109
(408) 540-6GFC [6432]
E-mail: info@girlsforachange.org
www.girlsforachange.org

Girls For A Change (GFC) is a national organization that empowers thousands of teen girls to create and lead social change. GFC provides girls with professional female role models, leadership training, and the inspiration to work together in teams to solve persistent societal problems in their communities.

GIRLS INCORPORATED

120 Wall Street
New York, NY 10005-3902
(212) 509-2000
Fax: (212) 509-8708
www.girlsinc.org

Girls Incorporated is a national nonprofit youth organization dedicated to inspiring all girls to be strong, smart, and bold. With roots dating to 1864, Girls Inc. has provided vital educational programs to millions of American girls, particularly those in high-risk, underserved areas. Today, innovative programs help girls confront subtle societal messages about their value and potential, and prepare them to lead successful, independent, and fulfilling lives.

GIRLS LEADERSHIP INSTITUTE

P.O. Box 50217
Baltimore, MD 21211
(410) 878-2258
Fax: (410) 558-6673
www.girlsleadershipinstitute.org/home2.htm

The mission of Girls Leadership Institute is to fight the crisis of confidence and dissociation that often oc-

curs in adolescent girls. When girls disconnect from their true feelings, their relationships become fraudulent, and they lose the ability to communicate what they really think and feel. The Institute believes that this loss of voice leads to a lifelong compromise of the quality of girls' relationships and leadership potential. The Institute's curriculum uses educational theater and is grounded in the research pioneered by psychologists Lyn Mikel Brown, Carol Gilligan, and their colleagues. The Institute's workshops empower girls to trace and resist the impact of "good girl" behaviors on their lives and relationships. The workshops teach skills to increase emotional intelligence during conflict, admit limitations and accept criticism, and connect the concept of "leadership" to everyday aspects of girls' lives.

GIRLS NATION & GIRLS STATE
GIRLS NATION

American Legion Auxiliary
National Headquarters
8945 N. Meridian Street
Indianapolis, IN 46260
(317) 569-4500
Fax: (317)-569-4502
E-mail: meetings@legion-aux.org
E-mail: alahq@legion-aux.org

GIRLS STATE

The National 4-H Conference Center
7100 Connecticut Ave.
Chevy Chase, MD 20815
http://girlsnation-auxiliary.com
www.legion-aux.org

Girls State is a nonpartisan program that teaches young women responsible citizenship and love for God and country. Since the inception of the Girls State program in 1937, nearly one million people have had the opportunity to learn first-hand how their state and local government works. High school girls who have completed their junior year spend an intensive week of study, working together as self-governing citizens at Auxiliary-sponsored Girls State programs in every state. They learn how to participate in the functioning of their state's government in preparation for their future roles as responsible citizens.

Two girls are selected from each Girls State program to attend Girls Nation, a national government training program. Girls Nation "senators" meet for a week in Washington, D.C., where they run for political office, campaign for the passage of legislation, and meet with state representatives and senators. Capping off the week of Girls Nation is a meeting with the president of the United States at the White House.

The Girls Nation program is funded by the national organization of the American Legion Auxiliary, with some support from each participating state. Little or no expense is required of the "senator" or her family. The American Legion Auxiliary believes that training our youth about the basic ideals and principles of our system of government will help to ensure the survival of our republic. Through this highly effective citizenship training program, Auxiliary members and other expert volunteers teach the youth of our nation to understand, comprehend, and appreciate their roles as United States citizens.

GOAL: Girls' Opportunities for Adventure and Leadership

124 Church Street
Decatur, GA 30030
(404) 214-1876
Fax: (404) 214-1888
E-mail: info@goalonline.org
www.goalonline.org

GOAL has developed an experiential curriculum that addresses the issues that middle school girls face and delivers high-quality, engaging programming at camps and weekend programs. All GOAL programs are predicated on the belief that the most profound learning begins with direct experience. All GOAL programs are structured in a way that moves girls through the "experiential learning cycle" from direct experience, to reflection, to generalizing, and finally to applying the knowledge to their own lives. By providing girl-specific, proactive programming that promotes self-esteem, self-awareness, and respect for individual differences to the girls of today, GOAL envisions a future generation of strong, competent, and resilient women, able to handle life's challenges with flexibility and a solid grounding in their own identity.

The Institute for Civic Leadership

Mills College
5000 MacArthur Blvd.
Oakland, CA 94613
(510) 430-3234
Fax: 510.430.3174
www.mills.edu/icl

The Institute for Civic Leadership promotes civic education and sponsors programs and activities that advance women's leadership. Women in their sophomore, junior, or senior year at Mills College or the University of California, Berkeley, are eligible to apply for the two-semester program in Civic Leadership. The course of study combines a discipline-based analysis of civic leadership and social policy with a personalized internship in which students work on public policy and social change projects. Students also receive mentoring from local women leaders, and participate in skill-building workshops and community-building activities.

Nestled in the foothills of Oakland, California, Mills College is a nationally renowned, independent liberal arts college offering a dynamic progressive education that fosters leadership, social responsibility, and creativity to approximately 950 undergraduate women and 500 graduate women and men. Since 2000, applications to Mills College have more than doubled. The College is named one of the top colleges in the West by *U.S. News & World Report*, one of the *Best 368 Colleges* by the Princeton Review, and ranks 75th among America's best colleges by Forbes.com. Visit us at www.mills.edu.

League of Women Voters

1730 M Street, NW, Suite 1000
Washington, DC 20036-4508
(202) 429-1965
Fax: (202) 429- 0854
www.lwv.org

The League of Women Voters, a nonpartisan political organization, has fought since 1920 to both improve our systems of government and impact public policies through citizen education and advocacy. The League is a decentralized, grassroots organization working at the national, state, and local levels.

There are Leagues in all 50 states, the District of Columbia, Puerto Rico, the Virgin Islands, and Hong Kong, in addition to the hundreds of local Leagues nationwide.

The League of Women Voters is strictly nonpartisan; it neither supports nor opposes candidates for office at any level of government. At the same time, the League is wholeheartedly political and works to influence policy through advocacy. Over time, the League's legislative priorities change to reflect the needs of society and critical issues of concern. The organization remains true to its basic purpose: to make democracy work for all citizens. The League of Women Voters makes a difference in the lives of citizens because of the energy and passion of thousands of members committed to the League's principles.

NATIONAL COUNCIL FOR RESEARCH ON WOMEN

11 Hanover Square, 24th Floor
New York, NY 10005
(212) 785-7335
Fax: (212) 785-7350
E-mail: ncrw@ncrw.org
www.ncrw.org

The National Council for Research on Women is a network of more than 100 leading U.S. research, advocacy, and policy centers with a growing global reach. The Council harnesses the resources of its network to ensure fully informed debate, policies, and practices to build a more inclusive and equitable world for women and girls.

NATIONAL ORGANIZATION FOR WOMEN

1100 H Street NW, 3rd Floor
Washington, DC 20005
(202) 628-8669 [628-8NOW]
Fax: (202) 785-8576
www.now.org

The National Organization for Women (NOW) is the largest organization of feminist activists in the United States. NOW has 500,000 contributing members and 550 chapters in all 50 states and the District of Columbia.

Since its founding in 1966, NOW's goal has been to take action to bring about equality for women. NOW works to eliminate discrimination and harassment in the workplace, schools, the justice system, and all other sectors of society; secure abortion, birth control, and reproductive rights for all women; end all forms of violence against women; eradicate racism, sexism, and homophobia; and promote equality and justice in our society.

NORTH CAROLINA CENTER FOR WOMEN IN PUBLIC SERVICE

P.O. Box 27421
Raleigh, NC 27611
(919) 508-2308
www.nccwps.org

The North Carolina Center for Women in Public Service is a nonpartisan, nonprofit organization that reaches across the state to:

- Prepare women to seek and serve in elected and appointed office,
- Advocate for systems and infrastructure that facilitate women's involvement, and
- Promote the value of women in governance.

Our long-term goal is to see the number of women in appointed and elected office be proportionate to the number of women who reside in this state. All of our programs, including the Women in Office Institute, 10 in 2010 series, and the Women on Board workshops, are open to women of all backgrounds, interests, and political affiliations. We strategically recruit for all our programs to ensure the participation of women of color and women from all areas of our state.

Sadie Nash Leadership Project

157 Montague Street, 4th Floor
Brooklyn, NY 11201
(718) 422-8664
www.sadienash.org

Sadie Nash Leadership Project was founded in 2001 to promote leadership and activism among young women. The program is designed to strengthen, empower, and equip young women as agents for change in their world. By increasing participation of women in social, political, and economic decision making, SNLP seeks to question and redefine the nature of leadership and to promote perspectives and practices that are cooperative, accountable, ethical, and effective.

Sue Shear Institute for Women in Public Life

University of Missouri – St. Louis
One University Blvd.
St. Louis, MO 63121-4400
(314) 516-4727
Fax: (314) 516-6621
http://www.umsl.edu/~iwpl

The Sue Shear Institute for Women in Public Life is a nonpartisan, educational organization that helps women break through the internal and external barriers to full participation in the public policy process. Founded in 1996, the Institute has offices at the University of Missouri in St. Louis and Kansas City. Program offerings include a campaign school for candidates and campaign workers, programs to facilitate the success of women in government and the judiciary, and a leadership academy for college students focused on women's public sector leadership.

Third Wave Foundation

25 East 21st Street, 4th Floor
New York, NY 10010
(212) 228-8311
Fax: (212) 780-9181
E-mail: info@thirdwavefoundation.org
www.thirdwavefoundation.org

Third Wave is a feminist, activist foundation that works nationally to support young women and transgender youth ages 15 to 30. Through grants, leadership development, and philanthropic advocacy, the Foundation supports groups and individuals working toward gender, racial, economic, and social justice.

Third Wave is led by a board of young women, men, and transgender activists striving to combat inequalities that they themselves face as a result of their age, gender, race, sexual orientation, economic status, or level of education. By empowering young women and transgender youth nationwide, Third Wave is building a lasting foundation for young feminists around the country. Third Wave envisions a world in which young women and transgender youth have the skills, power, and opportunity to engage in and lead efforts for social justice.

The White House Project

National Office
434 West 33rd Street, 8th Floor
New York, NY 10001
(212) 261-4400
Fax: (212) 904-1296
www.thewhitehouseproject.org

The White House Project (a Section 501 (c)(3) organization) aims to advance women's leadership in all communities and sectors—up to the U.S. presidency—by filling the leadership pipeline with a richly diverse, critical mass of women.

Women & Politics Institute

American University
4400 Massachusetts Avenue, NW
Ward 237
Washington, DC 20016
(202) 885-2903
Fax: 202-885-1305
E-mail: wandp@american.edu
http://wandp.american.edu

The Women & Politics Institute is located within the School of Public Affairs at American University.

Ranked among the top ten institutions of its kind by *U.S. News & World Report*, the School of Public Affairs prepares leaders for careers in public service. The Women & Politics Institute is one of the leading centers dedicated to research on women and politics and training the next generation of women leaders. The Women & Politics Institute's strategic location in Washington, D.C., allows students, faculty, and participants alike easy access to the resources of the nation's capital. The Institute's various training programs have given its participants and students the opportunity to explore various professional careers, develop strategies for advancing their careers, and form relationships with women leaders for mentoring and guidance.

WOMEN IN GOVERNMENT

1319 F Street, NW

Suite 710

Washington, DC 20004

(202) 333-0825

Fax: (202) 333-0875

www.womeningovernment.org/home

Women In Government is a national Section 501 (c)(3), nonprofit, bipartisan organization of women state legislators providing leadership opportunities, networking, expert forums, and educational resources to address and resolve complex public policy issues. Women In Government leads the nation with a bold, courageous, and passionate vision that empowers and mobilizes all women legislators to effect sound policy.

YOUNG DEMOCRATS OF AMERICA

910 17th Street, NW, Suite 215

Washington, DC 20006

(202) 639-8585

Fax: (202) 318-3221

E-mail: office@yda.org

MySpace: www.myspace.com/youngdems

YouTube: www.youtube.com/youngdems

The Young Democrats of America (YDA) is the largest youth-led partisan political organization that builds strong chapters and a solid youth voting bloc for Democrats nationwide. As the official youth arm of the Democratic Party, YDA mobilizes young people under the age of 36 to participate in the electoral process, influence the ideals of the Democratic Party, and develop the skills of their generation to serve as leaders at the local and national level.

YDA has 43 chartered states and U.S. territories with over 1,500 local chapters. YDA's 150,000-plus membership—including middle school, high school, and college students, as well as young workers, young professionals, and young families—reflects the broad diversity of our nation and the Democratic Party.

About The Editors And Photographer

AMY SEWELL is a writer and filmmaker with a passion for creating books and documentaries that are hopeful and inspirational. After writing and producing *Mad Hot Ballroom* (Paramount, 2005), Sewell made her directorial debut with the 2008 documentary *What's Your Point, Honey?*, about the current state of gender inequality at a pivotal time in political history. As a writer, she motivates others to leap into the world of filmmaking with her book, *The Mad Hot Adventures of an Unlikely Documentary Filmmaker* (Hyperion, 2007). Sewell is also the founder and director of *Give It Up for the ARTS!*, a nonprofit organization with the primary goal of exposing at-risk kids to the arts.

HEATHER L. OGILVIE has edited collections of essays by political, business, and financial leaders, for such publishers as Bloomberg Press and Thomson. She has edited books and periodicals in the fields of education, health, and business, and has an A.B. from Vassar College. Her 20-year career in publishing also includes considerable writing and ghostwriting experience, which she hopes will someday serve groundbreaking filmmakers, photographers, and future U.S. presidents.

Photo: Jan Audun Uretsky

ROBERT A. RIPPS has been shooting portraits and lifestyle images for magazines and corporate clients, as well as for advertising, for over 20 years. He has photographed over a thousand personalities including world leaders, actors, authors, business leaders, musicians, artists, and sports figures. He has won awards from both the PDN Photo/Design Awards, and the PDN/Nikon Self Promotion Awards. Robert has exhibited his work nationally, and his stock is licensed worldwide by Photonica/Getty, UpperCut Images, and Workbook Stock/Jupiter. Currently a Vice President on the National Board of the Advertising Photographers of America, Robert also is a member of ASMP (American Society of Media Photographers), EP (Editorial Photographers), SAA (Stock Artist Alliance), and the PLUS Coalition. He has a BFA in photography from Rochester Institute of Technology (RIT).

ACKNOWLEDGMENTS

Special Thanks

To Heather and Bob for sharing this journey with me. And as always, to my guy for hanging on to the string at the end of the balloon, and to my girls, who help keep that balloon in the air and soaring.

    —AMY SEWELL

To Andrea Brescia, Neill C. Furio, Pam Goett, Kevin Moran, and Jan Audun Uretsky for their expert advice and encouragement.

    —HEATHER L. OGILVIE

To Jill, for encouraging me to take the plunge; to my boys Max and Oliver—may you also have the dream, whatever it may be; to all my wonderful subjects, who gave me a chance to capture a glimmer of their souls—I hope you feel I got it right; and of course, my co-conspirators (and "assistants"), Amy and Heather, for giving me the opportunity to become a part of this adventure. To be continued....

    —ROBERT A. RIPPS